Step by Step Art 6 Worki the C

by Dianne Williams

CONTENTS

Section 1
Skills to Start With
(for Key Stage 1 pupils)

Section 2
Building on the Basics
(for Lower Key Stage 2 pupils)

Section 3
Extending the Ideas
(for Upper Key Stage 2 pupils)

Step by Step Art Books are available from all good Educational Bookshops and by mail order from:

Topical Resources, P.O. Box 329, Broughton, Preston, Lancashire. PR3 5LT

Topical Resouces publishes a range of Educational Materials for use in Primary Schools and Pre-School Nurseries and Playgroups.

For the latest catalogue:
Tel: 01772 863157
Fax: 01772 866153
e.mail: sales@topical-resources.co.uk
Visit our website: www.topical-resources.co.uk

Copyright © Dianne Williams

Printed in Great Britain for 'Topical Resources' by T. Snape & Company Ltd., Boltons Court, Preston, Lancashire.

Typeset by Paul Sealey Illustration & Design, 3 Wentworth Drive, Thornton, Lancashire.

First Published September 2002

ISBN 1 872977 72 3

Introduction

Most children are fascinated by computers - but many teachers are not! The magic of instant colour, marks and shapes that can be added to or undone instantly can be addictive, enjoyed and played with at the expense of the acquisition and progression of skills. This book is aimed to help teachers and the children they teach become familiar with the range of tools plus basic keyboard and mouse skills using the paint and drawing package 'Dazzle'. This is the only program referred to in the book. It seemed wiser to concentrate on just one program rather than try to describe several art packages, of which there are many and only add to the confusion! Most of the activities described could in fact successfully be used or adapted for other Art programs. If you already have a version of 'Dazzle' it may vary slightly from the one I have used i.e. in the range of tools on the tool bar, but the majority of the functions will be the same.

The book is divided into three sections - Skills to Start With (Key Stage One), Building on the Basics (Lower Key Stage Two), and Extending the Ideas (Upper Key Stage Two). Each section builds on the previous one and introduces new tools and their applications. The year groups indicated are suggestions only and teachers may feel they want to re-arrange or use the activities in a different order.

The book is similar to the other books in the 'Step by Step' series in that each activity has a 'Talk About' section, a 'Doing' section and a range of further suggestions to practise and use the skills introduced.

Many of the activities in the book link naturally to current practice in Art and Design using traditional media and they could therefore be used alongside an existing scheme of work to support, enrich and extend work in the classroom.

Although the book has an 'Art' focus most of the skills introduced will support other curriculum areas where the use of a computer is required or appropriate to meet the demands of the National Curriculum.

The aim of the book is to instill teacher confidence in introducing and using an Art package with their children who hopefully in turn will learn to select tools with confidence and understanding, use their imagination and become creative with the medium of computer technology.

Finally I should like to thank my friend and colleague Michelle Singleton for her help, encouragement and support in producing this book. Without her extensive computer knowledge and expertise, the task would have been far more daunting and difficult.

Dianne Williams

Dazzle, as well as other titles in the **Step by Step Art** series is available through: Topical Resources, P.O. Box 329, Broughton, Preston PR3 5LT.
Tel 01772 863158
Fax 01772 866153
email: sales@topical-resources.co.uk

Section 1: Skills to Start With (for Key Stage 1 pupils)

Teacher's Notes

In this section you will be using the 'Shapes and Spray Toolbar' with the 'Thin Strip' Colour Palette.

The Shapes and Spray Toolbar

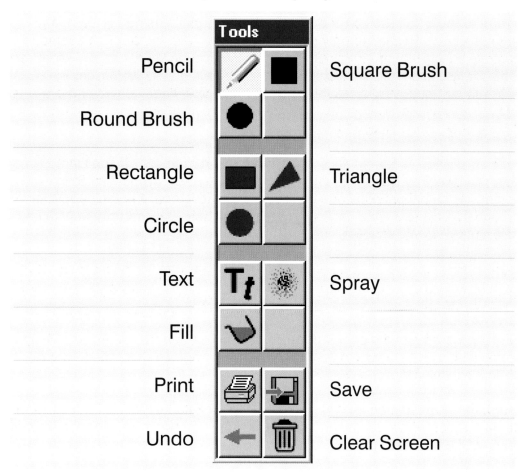

Pencil — Square Brush
Round Brush
Rectangle — Triangle
Circle
Text — Spray
Fill
Print — Save
Undo — Clear Screen

How to select the Shapes and Spray Toolbar

- The program Dazzle should be open on the screen.
- At the top left hand side of the screen you will see the word **Customize**.
- Using the left hand mouse button click on the word **Customize** and a drop down menu will appear.
- From the drop down menu click on the words **Custom files** and a box will appear on the screen (Example 1)

- Click on the small black down arrow next to the word **Dazzle** and a drop down menu will appear.
- From this drop down menu, using the left hand mouse button, click on **Shapes and Spray**, (this will now be highlighted in dark blue).
- Click on the button to the right of the menu labelled **load**.
- The toolbar will now change to the Shapes and Spray toolbar shown above.

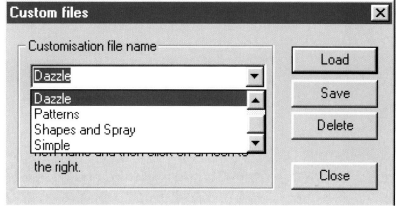

Example 1

The Thin Strip Colour Palette

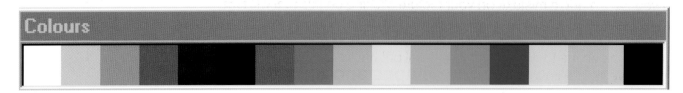

How to select the Thin Strip Colour Palette

- Click on the word **Customize** at the top left corner of the screen.
- From the drop down menu, select **colours** the following window will appear (Example 2).
- Click on the small black downward pointing arrow and a drop down menu will appear showing you a choice of different palettes.
- Click on the name of the palette you wish to use e.g. **Thin strip**. The Thin Strip Palette shown above, will appear on your screen.
- Left click on the blue area above the palette and drag it to a convenient working position.

Example 2

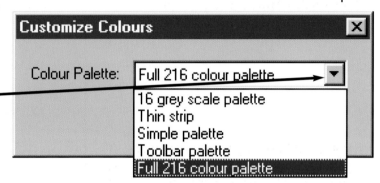

WHAT DO YOU ALSO NEED TO KNOW?

- How to rub your work out
- How to undo a mistake
- How to start again with a clear screen
- How to save your work
- How to print your work

How to rub out

There is no icon on the toolbar, which is for rubbing out the image. The simplest method for creating a rubber is....

- Choose the colour white from the colour palette.
- Select either the square or the circle tool. Draw with the tool which will perform like a rubber by covering the colour with white.

How to undo a mistake

- If you have made a mistake on your picture clicking on this tool will take out the very last action, which you carried out. It will not undo the entire picture.
- If you click on the tool a second time it will put back the image, which you have just taken away.

How to clear the screen

- If you want to start again with a clear screen click on the **dustbin** found on the toolbox.
- Click on the '**Throw away**' button.
- A clear page will now appear.

How to print your work

- If you want to print your work, click on the icon opposite, or choose **Print** from the **File** menu.
- A window will appear telling you which printer you are attached to.
- Click on the **OK** button at the bottom of this window to start the printing process.

You can change the way the image is printed out on the page to make the most of the page size. To do this simply click on the button labelled **Properties** from the window, which has just appeared.

- The window opposite will appear (Example 3): From here you can select how you want your picture to appear on the page, landscape or portrait. Click inside the small circle at the side of the picture to make your choice.

- Click on the **OK** button at the bottom of the window and click on the OK button in the print window to start the printing process.

Work can be saved and retrieved from the hard disk in the normal manner.

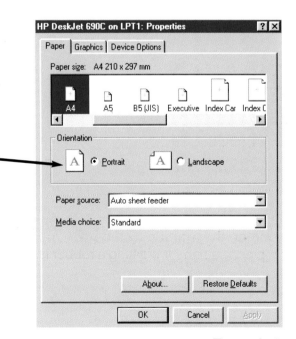

Example 3

How to save your work to a floppy disc

- Insert a floppy disc into your disc drive.
- If you want to save your work, click on the icon opposite.
- A 'Save As' window will appear showing you where your image will be saved. Click on the small black downward pointing arrow. (Example 4)
- From the list, which appears, choose **Floppy (A)**.
- In the box next to '**File name**' type in a name for your image. Remember to keep the name simple, avoid using any punctuation or spaces in the name which you choose. For my example I have chosen, 'apples'.
- Click on the **Save** button at the side of the file name.

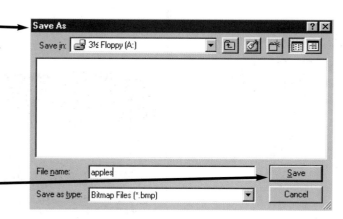

Example 4

You could use the child's surname followed by the name of the picture e.g. Jonesrainbow. This makes it simpler for the teacher to identify the images and to whom they belong.

How to reload your image from a floppy disc

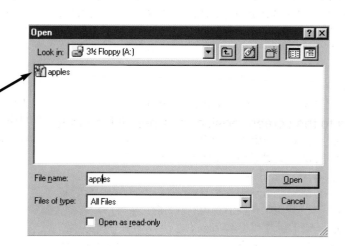

- Insert the floppy disc into your disc drive.
- Click on the icon opposite.
- An open window will appear. Click on the small black downward pointing arrow. (Example 5)
- From the list which appears select the area where you saved your work i.e. **Floppy (A)**.
- The names of the files stored on the disc will appear in the space below. Click on the name of the file you want to open, and then click on the **open** button at the bottom of the window.
- The image will now appear on the page.

Example 5

Making Marks

Tools to Use:

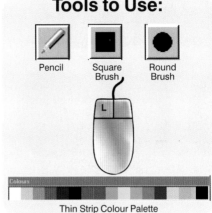

Pencil   Square   Round
          Brush   Brush

Thin Strip Colour Palette

Talk About
- The name of each tool to be used.
- What each tool icon looks like.
- Where each tool is found on the tool bar and where its name appears (at the bottom left side of the screen) when the tool is clicked on.
- Clicking on a tool icon with the left mouse button, moving to the screen, positioning the icon that appears, clicking again and then moving the mouse around to begin drawing.
- Clicking with the left mouse button to stop drawing and returning to the tool bar to select a new tool.
- Repeating the same sequence each time a new tool is selected.

Doing
- Click on the pencil tool with the left mouse button, return to the screen, position the pencil icon that appears, click with the left hand mouse button, hold it down, and drag the mouse to draw a line. Click to finish the line.
- Click on the square brush tool with the left mouse button, return to the screen, position the square and brush icon that appears, click with the left mouse button, hold it down, and drag the mouse to draw a line. Click to finish the line.
- Click on the round brush tool with the left mouse button, return to the screen, position the circle and brush icon that appears, click with the left mouse button, hold it down and drag the mouse to draw a line. Click to finish the line.

Extending the Activity
- Click on each of the drawing tools in turn and draw the same sort of line with each one e.g. a line with a loop in it.
- Click on each of the drawing tools in turn and draw a different sort of line with each one e.g. a zig-zag line, a curly line and a wavy line.
- Draw lines that go in different directions e.g. diagonally, horizontally etc.
- The children could work in pairs, one child choosing a drawing tool, beginning a line and then clicking on any tool to finish. The second child then needs to find the tool that has been used, click on it, return to the screen and continue adding to the line.
- The children could be given written or drawn examples of the lines they are to draw and the tool they must use to draw each one.
- The children could work in a similar way using a range of traditional drawing media.

Thick & Thin Lines

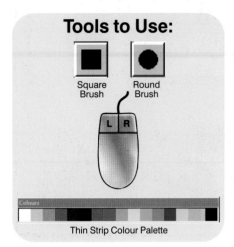

Tools to Use:

Square Brush

Round Brush

Colours

Thin Strip Colour Palette

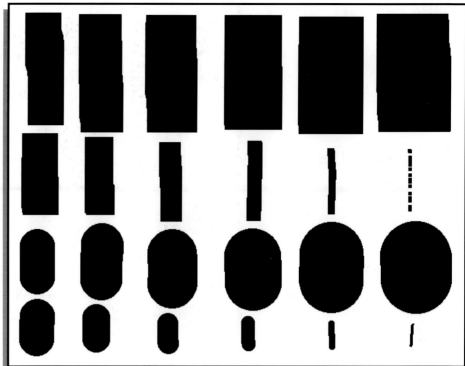

Talk About
- What thick and thicker mean.
- What thin and thinner mean.
- Which is the left-hand mouse button and which is the right button.
- The up arrow to click on to make lines thicker.
- The down arrow to click on to make lines thinner.
- The starting point that appears in the box is normally 50 pt.

Doing
Click on the square brush icon on the tool bar with the right mouse button.
- A window will appear with the word 'Brush' at the top, the size of the brush (50 pt) plus upward and downward pointing arrows.
- The upward arrow will increase the size of the brush when it is clicked on with the left mouse button.
- The downward arrow will decrease the size of the brush if it is clicked on with the left mouse button.
- The changing size of the brush will appear as a square next to the size window.
- To keep an altered brush size in order to draw with it, click on 'close'. The new brush size is now ready to draw with.
- Use the square brush icon, increase the thickness of it, click on close and draw a line with it.
- Make it thicker still and draw another line. Continue making the brush thicker and drawing a new line each time.

- Repeat the activity but this time make the brush thinner for each line.
- Click on the round brush icon with the right mouse button and follow the same instructions as you did with the square brush.

Extending the Activity
- Draw the thickest line you can make with the square brush, and then the thinnest line.
- Draw the thickest line you can make with the round brush, and then the thinnest line.
- Use the square brush, start at 50 pt and draw a row of vertical lines making each one thicker than the one before.
- Use the square brush, start at 50 pt and draw a row of vertical lines making each one thinner than the one before.
- Repeat the same activity using the round brush.
- Draw a row of lines that are a mixture i.e. thick and thin using both brushes. Try the same activity with traditional drawing media e.g. a pencil and a crayon.

Squares and Dots

Tools to Use:

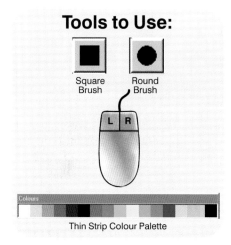

Square Brush   Round Brush

L R

Colours

Thin Strip Colour Palette

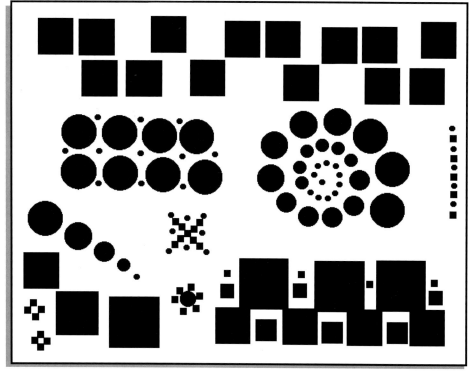

Talk About
- What a dot looks like and what a square looks like.
- The brush on the tool bar that will make squares - the square brush.
- The brush on the toolbar that will make dots - the round brush.
- Which is the left mouse button and which is the right button.
- The up arrow to click on to make the dots and squares bigger.
- The down arrow to click on to make the dots and squares smaller.
- How to get the box to change the size of the dots and squares (see page 8).
- How to keep a new size of dot or square to draw with (see page 8).

Doing
- Click on the square brush icon on the toolbar with the left mouse button and then go to the screen.
- A square and a brush will appear, click on the screen and a square will be drawn. Move the mouse, click again and you will get another square. If you drag the mouse rather than clicking it, you will get a line and not a square. Click and draw several squares of the same size on different parts of the screen.

- Next click on the round brush icon on the tool bar with the left mouse button and go to the screen.
- A circle and a brush will appear. Click on the screen and a dot will be drawn. Move the mouse and click again and you will get another dot. If you drag the mouse rather than clicking it you will get a line and not a dot. Click and draw several dots of the same size on different parts of the screen.

Extending the Activity
- Make a pattern of alternating squares and dots.
- Click on the square brush icon on the tool bar with the right mouse button, you will have opened the window with the arrows to make the squares larger and smaller. Change the size of the square. Click on close to keep the size.
- Explore changing the size of the squares. Make patterns of large and small squares.
- Change the size of the dots in the same way and make patterns of large and small dots.
- Make patterns of dots and squares of different sizes.

Lines, Dots & Squares

Tools to Use:

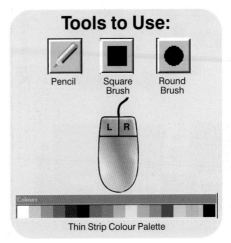

Pencil Square Brush Round Brush

L R

Colours

Thin Strip Colour Palette

Talk About
- Which is the left mouse button and which is the right.
- When to use the left mouse button and what it will do.
- When to use the right mouse button and what it will do.
- The up arrow that makes a line or dot larger and the down arrow that makes a line or dot smaller.
- How to keep the new size of line, dot or square in order to draw with it (click on 'Close').
- How to draw a line, a dot and a square.
- The fact that the width of the lines drawn with a pencil cannot be changed.

Doing
- Click on the square brush icon with the right mouse button, change the width of the line i.e. make it either bigger or smaller with the left mouse button, click on close and return to the screen.
- Click and drag to draw a pattern of lines with the brush. Leave gaps between the lines.
- Return to the tool bar, click on the square brush icon with the right mouse button, change the width of the line with the left button, click on close and return to the screen.
- Click and drag to add lines in this new width to your pattern - they could go across, between or around the first group of lines you drew.

- Try the same activity using the round brush.
- Add some fine lines to your patterns using the pencil tool on the tool bar - click on the pencil tool icon with the left mouse button, move to the screen, click and drag to draw the fine lines.
- Add some dots or squares to your pattern - they could be large or small, or both.

Extending the Activity
- Draw a pattern of thick horizontal lines and thin vertical lines.
- Draw a pattern of dots of different sizes. Surround each dot with pencil lines.
- Draw a criss-cross group of lines like a star; add a small dot to the end of each line.
- Draw several horizontal lines of different widths; add a square to the end of each one. Make each square a different size.
- Draw several horizontal wavy lines of different widths under each other. Leave gaps between the lines. Add rows of dots of different sizes between the lines.
- Draw a new pattern that uses different sizes of lines, squares and dots.
- Draw similar patterns using a range of traditional drawing media.

Coloured Lines and Squares

Tools to Use:

Square Brush

Thin Strip Colour Palette

Talk About
- The number of colours on the thin strip palette.
- The name of each of the colours on the thin strip palette.
- Clicking on a colour with the left mouse button to select it.
- Where the selected colour appears (in a box at the end of the thin strip palette).
- Changing to a new colour by clicking on it with the left mouse button.
- How to move the thin strip palette if it hides part of the screen to be drawn (see below).
- How to draw a line and how to draw a square.

Doing
- Move the cursor on to one of the coloured squares on the thin strip palette at the bottom of the screen and click the left mouse button. The box at the end of the palette will now change to the colour you have chosen.
- Move the cursor on to each of the colours in turn, click and watch the end box change colour.
- Explore moving the thin strip palette to different parts of the screen as follows: Place the cursor on the blue strip at the top of the palette - it has the word 'Colours' on it. Click the left mouse button anywhere on the blue strip, hold and drag the strip to another part of the screen. Move the palette to the top of the screen, then to the left, then the right and finally to the bottom of the screen.

- Click on a colour then click on the square brush icon on the tool bar with the left mouse button. Return to the screen, a square and brush appears, click the left mouse button and you will get a square in the colour you chose.
- Click on a new colour, move to a different part of the screen, click again and another square in the new colour will appear.
- Use each of the colours in turn and draw a row of different coloured squares along the top of the screen.
- Now draw some lines with the square brush. Draw each line in a different colour.

Extending the Activity
- Draw a pattern of different coloured lines. Move the colour bar when you need to.
- Draw a pattern of different coloured squares. Move the colour bar when you need to.
- Draw a pattern using both lines and squares of different colours. Move the colour bar when you need to.
- Draw a similar pattern using either thin wax crayons or felt tip pens in assorted colours on squared maths paper.

Coloured Lines & Dots

Tools to Use:

Round Brush

Colours

Thin Strip Colour Palette

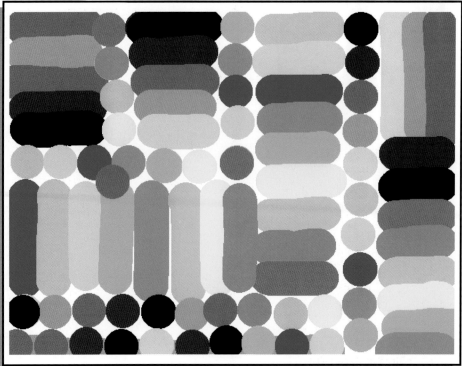

Talk About
- The number and names of the colours on the thin strip palette.
- How to change a colour by moving the cursor on to a different colour and clicking the left mouse button.
- Where the new colour appears.
- How to move the thin strip palette around the screen if it hides part of the screen to be drawn on.
- How to draw a line and how to draw a dot.

Doing
- Move the cursor on to one of the coloured squares on the thin strip palette at the bottom of the screen and click the left mouse button. The box at the end of the palette will now change to the colour you clicked on.
- Move the cursor on to each of the colours in turn, click and watch the end box change colour.
- Explore moving the thin strip colour palette to different parts of the screen by placing the cursor on the blue strip at the top of the palette - it has the word colours on it. Click the left-hand mouse button, hold and drag the strip to another part of the screen.
- Try moving the colour palette from side to side and up and down the screen.
- Click on a colour, then click on the round brush icon on the tool bar with the left mouse button. Return to the screen, a circle and a brush will appear. Click the left mouse button and you will get a dot in the chosen colour.

- Click on a new colour, move to a different part of the screen, click again and another dot in the new colour will appear.
- Use each of the colours in turn and draw a row of different coloured dots along the top of the screen.
- Now draw some lines with the round brush. Draw each line in a different colour.

Extending the Activity
- Draw a pattern of different coloured lines. Move the colour bar when needed.
- Draw a pattern of different coloured dots. Move the colour bar when needed.
- Draw a pattern using both lines and dots of different colours. Move the colour bar when you need to.
- Draw a pattern using both the square brush and the round brush using lines dots and squares of different colours.
- Draw a similar pattern using either thin wax crayons or felt tip pens in assorted colours on squared maths paper.

Changing Colours & Tools

Tools to Use:

Pencil   Square Brush   Round Brush

L

Colours

Thin Strip Colour Palette

Talk About

- The different tools to use, what they are called and where they are found on the tool bar.
- How to choose each tool and how to change tools by clicking on them with the left mouse button before moving on to the screen.
- How to change colours by moving the cursor on to a new colour and clicking the left mouse button.
- How to draw lines, how to draw dots and how to draw squares.
- How to move the colour bar to a different part of the screen so that it doesn't hide the part you are working on.
- Using all the tools and lots of different colours for your work.

Doing

- Practise changing tools and using the tools in different ways i.e. for lines, squares and dots.
- Practise changing colours and moving the tool bar.
- To get rid of your 'practice' work and to clear the screen, click on the dustbin icon on the tool bar with the left mouse button.
- A box will appear on the screen - there are two strips in it. One says 'Throw Away', the other says 'Cancel'. Click on Throw Away with the left mouse button and the screen will clear.
- You are now ready to draw and cover the screen with dots, squares and lines in different colours using the different tools.
- Try drawing squares on one part of the screen, dots on another and lines on another. Leave gaps between the lines, dots and squares.
- Fill these gaps with other lines, dots and squares.
- Use the pencil to draw thin lines, patterns and shapes on top of the thick lines, dots and squares.
- Try putting dots and squares on top of the thick lines.
- Try putting dots on top of squares. You need to use two colours for this.
- If you draw a line, square or dot you don't want to keep you can get rid of it by clicking with the left mouse button on the Undo tool on the tool bar. This will only undo one mark i.e. the last one you made.

Extending the Activity

- Draw a design that is similar but only use three colours.
- Draw a design that has groups of squares surrounded by dots with lines around the edge. Add extra drawn shapes and lines for decoration.
- Draw a design that has a large group of dots in the centre, surround these with lines and finally with squares. Add extra shapes and lines for decoration.
- Draw a similar pattern using a range of traditional coloured drawing media.

Using the Fill Tool

Tools to Use:

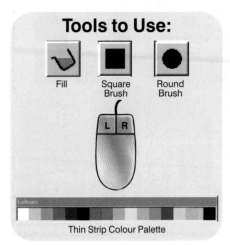

Fill   Square   Round
          Brush   Brush

L R

Thin Strip Colour Palette

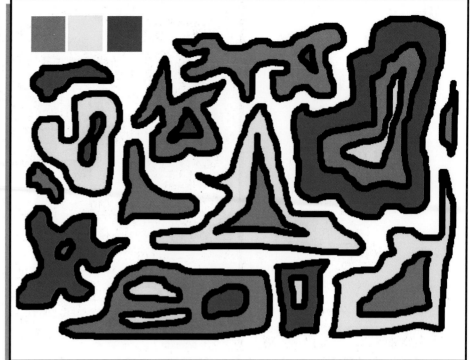

Talk About

- What the fill tool looks like and where it is found on the tool bar.
- How to activate the fill tool by clicking on it with the left mouse button.
- How to fill an area or shape on the screen with colour i.e. clicking on a colour then moving the cursor on to the area or shape and clicking on it with the left mouse button.
- How to make the round brush thinner (see page 8).
- Drawing shapes with the round brush, and making sure that the outline of each shape is complete and has no gaps. (If there are gaps the colour when added will flood into the surrounding area as well.)
- Using only Primary colours. What the Primary colours are i.e. red, yellow and blue; and where they are found on the thin strip colour palette.

Doing

- Click on one of the primary colours with the left mouse button. Click on the square brush icon on the toolbar with the left mouse button and return to the screen.
- Move the brush and square that appear to the top of the screen, click and a square of your chosen colour will appear.
- Repeat this with the other two primary colours, clicking and drawing squares of each one at the top of the screen.
- Go to the round brush icon on the tool bar, use the left and right mouse buttons as before and reduce the size of the brush to 10pt.

- Click on close with the left mouse button and return to the screen.
- Click on black on the thin strip palette with the left mouse button and draw several different shapes by holding and dragging the mouse to create the outline of each one.
- Make sure each outline is complete before letting go of the mouse button and moving to a different part of the screen clicking and beginning another shape.
- To fill each shape in turn, click on the fill tool, then click on one of the primary colours, move the icon to the middle of the shape and click .The shape should now fill with the colour you chose.
- If the whole screen fills with the colour as well it is because there is a gap in the outline, click on the undo icon on the tool bar, return to the round brush, draw over the outline of the shape and try filling it again.
- Use a different primary colour each time.

Extending the Activity

- Fill each of the shapes you have drawn with a different colour.
- Draw the outline of each shape in a different colour. Fill them all with the same colour, or fill each one with a different colour.
- Draw or paint similar shapes and fill them with Primary colours only.

Filling with Warm Colours

Tools to Use:

Fill   Round Brush

L | R

Colours

Thin Strip Colour Palette

Talk About

- Which colours are called warm colours and the warm colours that can be found on the thin strip palette - red, brown, orange and yellow.
- Using only these colours to fill the shapes you draw and the background.
- Making the round brush thinner as on page 8. Reduce it to 10 pt.
- Drawing a shape with lots of loops and circles in it that fills the screen.
- Making sure the outline of each loop or circle is complete and has no gaps.
- If there are gaps or you touch the outline - the screen fills! Use the Undo tool if this happens.

Doing

- Go to the round brush icon on the tool bar, use the left and right mouse buttons as before and reduce the size of the brush to 10pt.
- Click on black on the thin strip palette with the left mouse button and use the brush and circle icon, now on the screen, to draw a large shape full of loops and circles.
- If you want to start again, click on the dustbin icon on the toolbar with the left mouse button. The words 'Throw Away' and 'Cancel' will appear, click on Throw away with the left-hand mouse button and the screen will clear.

- To get rid of the last mark you drew click on the Undo tool on the tool bar.
- When your shape is ready, fill the loops and circles in it, one at time with different warm colours. Start by using the left mouse button to click on a warm colour on the palette, then click on the fill tool icon, return to the loop or circle to be filled and click on it. It should now fill with the colour you chose. Use the same colour to fill several different parts of your drawing before changing to another warm colour.
- To change to a new colour, click on another warm colour on the palette with the left mouse button then click on the next area to be filled.
- To fill the background, click on a colour and then click on the area around the outside of your drawing.
- You can undo your last colour fill using the Undo tool as before or by filling the shape with a new colour on top of the original one.

Extending the Activity

- Draw a shape made up of overlapping circles.
- Draw a shape with a specific number of loops in it.
- Draw or paint similar shapes and fill them with warm colours only.

15

Filling with Cold Colours

Tools to Use:

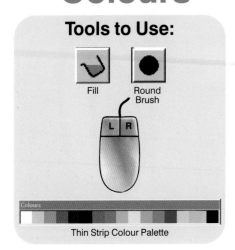

Fill   Round Brush

Thin Strip Colour Palette

Talk About

- Which colours are called cold colours and the cold colours that can be found on the thin strip palette - blue, turquoise and grey. (Use only one of the greys).
- Using only these colours to fill the shapes you draw and the background.
- Making the round brush thinner as on page 8. Reduce it to 10 pt.
- Drawing a shape with lots of spikes and triangles in it that fills the screen.
- Making sure the outline of each spike or triangle is complete and has no gaps.
- If there are gaps or if you touch the outline - the screen fills! Use the Undo tool if this happens.

Doing

- Go to the round brush icon on the tool bar, use the left and right mouse buttons as before and reduce the size of the brush to 10 pt.
- Click on black on the thin strip palette with the left mouse button and use the brush and circle icon, now on the screen, to draw a large shape made up of spikes and triangles.
- If you want to start again, click on the dustbin icon on the left-hand tool bar with the left-hand mouse button. The words 'Throw Away' and 'Cancel' will appear, click on Throw Away with the left mouse button and the screen will clear.
- To get rid of the last mark you drew, click on the Undo tool on the tool bar.
- When your shape is ready, fill the spikes and triangles in it, one at a time with different cold colours. Start by using the left mouse button to click on a cold colour on the palette, then click on the fill tool icon on the left tool bar. Return to the spike or triangle to be filled and click on it. It should now fill with the colour you chose. Use the same colour to fill several parts of your drawing before changing to another cold colour.
- To change to a new colour, click on another cold colour on the palette with the left mouse button then click on the next area to be filled.
- To fill the background, click on a colour and then click on the area around the outside of your drawing.
- You can undo your last colour fill using the Undo tool as before or by filling the shape with a new colour on top of the original one.

Extending the Activity

- Draw a shape made up of overlapping triangles.
- Draw a shape with a specific number of spikes.
- Draw groups of large and small triangles to fill with cold colours.
- Draw or paint similar shapes and fill them with cold colours only.

Using the Spray Gun

Tools to Use:

Spray

Thin Strip Colour Palette

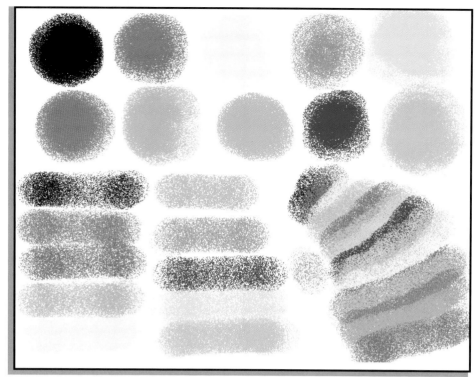

Talk About

- What the spray gun icon looks like, where it is found on the tool bar and how to click on and select the spray gun.
- Dragging the mouse to create a light spray of colour.
- Dragging over the top of the first spray to create a deeper colour.
- Combining colours i.e. using one colour first, then changing to a second colour and going over the first.
- How to change to a new colour.
- Drawing lines and circles with the spray gun.

Doing

- Click on the spray gun icon on the tool bar with the left mouse button. Return to the screen and go to the thin strip palette.
- Position the cursor arrow that appears on the colour that you want to work with and click the left mouse button.
- Return to a blank part of the screen, a circle and a brush will appear, click the left mouse button hold and drag the mouse to draw a line or circle.
- Try drawing faint lines by dragging once, and darker lines by dragging again over the top of the first line.
- Try drawing faint circles by dragging once, and circles with darker centres by dragging over the centre of the circle a second time.

- Click on a new colour with the left mouse button and repeat the activity i.e. drawing both lines and circles.
- Use all the colours from the black to the end of the thin strip palette to draw individual lines and circles.
- Next try drawing a line in one colour first and then over drawing in a second colour.
- Give a name to each new shade you make.
- Repeat this activity but this time draw a circle using one colour on top of another.
- Give a name to each new shade you make.

Extending the Activity

- Fill the screen with lines, some in one colour and some in two. Make some of the lines faint and some of them dark.
- Fill the screen with circles, some in one colour and some in two. Make some of the circles faint and some of them dark.
- Fill the screen with lines and circles in the strong colours e.g. black, brown, red, orange, dark green and blue. Then draw over the top of each one in a paler colour e.g. yellow, light green, turquoise, pink and a pale grey.
- Repeat this activity using the colours the other way around; light then dark.
- Try this using one colour of wax crayon first and then blending another on top.

Sprayed Flowers

Tools to Use:

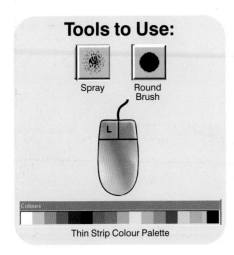

Spray   Round Brush

Thin Strip Colour Palette

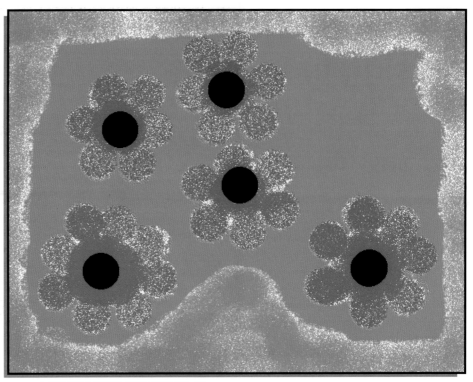

Talk About

- The tools that are going to be used, where they are on the tool bar, how to get a tool and how to change to a new tool.
- Which colours to use, where these colours are on the thin strip palette, how to get a colour and how to change to a new colour.
- The shape of 'daisy-like' flowers.
- Dragging the mouse to draw a circle to start the flower shape, clicking the mouse to draw each petal. Dragging or clicking over the top of a shape to make the colour deeper.
- Clicking the round brush tool to draw the centre of each flower.
- Using the fill tool to flood and fill the background.

Doing

- Click on the spray gun icon on the tool bar with the left mouse button, return to the screen and position the cursor arrow on the colour red and click.
- Return to the screen, position the circle and brush icon that appears to draw the first flower shape, click the left mouse button, hold it down and drag the mouse in a circle to draw the start of the flower shape. Drag over this same shape several times if you want to make the colour more intense.
- Let go of the left mouse button, move and position the brush and circle icon on the edge of the circle you have drawn, click the left mouse button, then let go to create a curved petal shape. Move round the edge of the circle, clicking and letting go to

create further petals. Click over each petal several times if you want to make the colour more intense.
- Draw more flowers in the same way before going to the round brush icon on the tool bar, clicking with the left mouse button returning to the screen clicking on the colour black then moving and clicking in the centre of each flower head with the left mouse button.
- Now go to the dark green colour on the thin strip palette, click with the left mouse button, move the brush and circle icon to the edge of the screen, click, drag and hold down the left mouse button and draw a shape around the edge of the screen. Drag over the shape several times if you want to make the colour darker. Finally go to the fill tool on the toolbar and click on it with the left mouse button. Return to the screen and click on the white area in the middle with the left mouse button. This area should now fill with dark green leaving the border a paler sprayed green.

Extending the Activity

- Draw a similar group of flowers using three different colours.
- Draw a similar group of flowers but make each flower a different colour.
- Make observational pencil drawings of flowers and plants.

Drawing Feathers

Tools to Use:

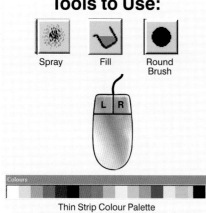

Spray   Fill   Round Brush

Thin Strip Colour Palette

Talk About

- The tools to be used, where they are on the toolbar, how to get a tool and how to change to a new tool.
- How to reduce the size of the round brush.
- The colours of the feathers and where these colours are on the thin strip palette. The shapes of the feathers - how they are wider at the bottom and narrower at the top.
- Adding lines to the feathers once the shapes and the colours are complete. Start with the long central line, then add the shorter lines branching out.

Doing

- Click on the fill tool icon on the left hand tool bar with the left mouse button, return to the screen, move to the thin strip palette and position the cursor arrow on the dark blue colour, click the left mouse button, return to the screen and click the left mouse button again and the screen will become blue.
- Go to the spray gun icon on the toolbar, click the left mouse button, and return to the screen.
- Go to the thin strip palette and position the cursor arrow on white, click the left mouse button, return to the screen and use the circle and brush icon that appears to draw several feather shapes on different parts of the screen.
- Do this by clicking, holding and dragging the mouse to draw each shape. Click to finish a shape before moving and clicking to start a new one. Now go to a grey, click, return to each feather,

click, let go and give each a little spray of grey up the centre.
- If you want to get rid of a drawing, either click on the Undo tool on the tool bar or click on the round brush icon, then click on the blue you used to fill the screen on the thin strip palette and use the brush and circle icon to draw over and hide what you want to get rid of.
- Go to the round brush icon again and use the right and left mouse buttons as on page 8 to reduce the size of the brush down to 5 pt. Position the cursor on black, click the left mouse button, then move to the first feather and begin adding lines. Click the left mouse button to finish a line and click it again to begin a new one. Finally click the left-hand mouse button on a pale grey on the palette, return to the screen, click and in the same way as before add grey lines to each feather. Add white lines to each in a similar way.

Extending the Activity

- Draw a similar group of feathers using three different colours.
- Draw a similar group of feathers but make each feather a different colour.
- Make observational pencil drawings of actual feathers.

Drawing Leaves

Tools to Use:

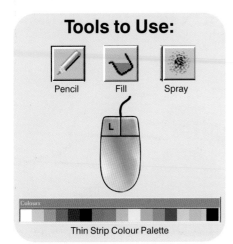

Pencil   Fill   Spray

Thin Strip Colour Palette

Talk About

- The tools to be used, where they are on the tool bar, how to get a tool and how to change to a new tool.
- The colours of autumn leaves and where these colours are on the thin strip palette.
- The shapes of the leaves - where they are wide and where they are narrow. Where the veins are, where they start and finish and how they branch out.
- Adding lines to the leaves, around the edge and also the stem and veins once the shapes and colours are complete. Start with the outline first and add the inner lines later.

Doing

- Click on the spray gun icon on the tool bar with the left mouse button and return to the screen. Go to the colour palette, position the cursor arrow on brown, click the left mouse button, return to the screen and use the circle and brush icon that appears to draw several leaf shapes on different parts of the screen. Do this by clicking, holding and dragging the mouse to draw each shape. Click to finish a shape before moving and clicking to start a new one.
- Go to the colour red on the palette, click the left mouse button, return to each leaf in turn, click, let go and give each one a spray of red. Go to the colour orange on the palette and click the left

mouse button, return to each leaf in turn, click, let go and give each a spray of orange. Go to the colour yellow on the palette and click the left mouse button, return to each leaf in turn, click, let go and give each a spray of yellow. Add more of these colours in the same way if you want to deepen the colour of the leaves.
- Go to the pencil tool icon on the tool bar, click on it with the left mouse button and return to the screen. Go to the colour palette and position the cursor arrow on black, click the left mouse button, return to the screen and use the pencil that appears to draw around the edge of each leaf. Give each one a central stalk and veins branching out from the centre. Hold down the left mouse button to draw each line.
- Go to the fill tool icon on the tool bar, click the left mouse button, return to the screen, move to the colour palette, position the cursor arrow on yellow, click left return to the screen, click again and the area around the leaves will fill with yellow.

Extending the Activity

- Draw a similar group of leaves but use the two greens plus yellow and brown.
- Draw a multi-coloured group of leaves.
- Make an observational drawing of a leaf carefully matching the colours.

Solid Shapes

Tools to Use:

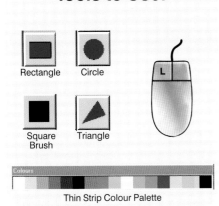

Rectangle   Circle

Square Brush   Triangle

Thin Strip Colour Palette

Talk About

- The difference between an outline shape and a solid shape. Where the solid shapes are on the tool bar and the name of each shape.
- How to click on and get a shape to use. Drawing each shape several times in different sizes. How to make each shape large or small by clicking and then dragging the mouse outwards, upwards or backwards whilst drawing the shape.
- Using just the Primary colours - one colour for each type of shape e.g. red for circles. What the primary colours are and where they are found on the thin strip palette.

Doing

- Click on the square brush icon on the tool bar with the left mouse button. Return to the screen, position the cursor arrow on red on the thin strip palette, click the left mouse button, move the brush and square icon that appears to the top of the screen, click and a red square will be drawn. Click on the yellow and blue in turn and add these as squares next to the red one.
- Click on red with the left mouse button, then click on the filled circle icon on the tool bar with the same button, return to the screen, a cross will appear. Click, let go and drag the mouse. A filled red circle will begin to take shape. Click to finish the drawing and to keep the size of circle you have drawn. Move the cross to another part of the screen, click and drag out a second circle. Continue drawing circles of different sizes.

- Click on blue with the left mouse button, then click on the filled triangle icon on the toolbar with the same button and return to the screen. A cross will appear. Click, a line appears, drag it to the length you want, click, the line disappears, drag, in a different direction and a filled triangle will start to take shape. Click to finish and keep the shape. Move the cross to another part of the screen, click and drag out a second triangle. Continue drawing triangles of different sizes.
- Click on yellow with the left mouse button, then click on the filled rectangle icon on the toolbar with the same button and return to the screen. A cross appears. Click, let go and drag. Depending how far you drag a filled square or rectangle will take shape. Click to finish and keep the shape. Move to another part of the screen, click and drag out a second square or rectangle. Continue drawing squares and rectangles of different sizes.

Extending the Activity

- Draw a row using all the shapes, the different sizes and different colours.
- Combine shapes on and next to each other to make new shapes e.g. a tree.
- Print similar shapes in Primary colours using boxes and lids.

Solid Shape Cat

Tools to Use:

Triangle Circle

Round Brush Fill

Colours

Thin Strip Colour Palette

Talk About
- Drawing one shape, then drawing a second shape to join and touch it to make a new shape.
- Drawing shapes on top of other shapes using different colours.
- The shapes that need to be combined to make the shape of a cat, e.g. the head, ears etc.
- Where to find these shapes and how to get them from the toolbar.
- Drawing these shapes in different sizes and colours.
- Reducing the size of the round brush using both the left and right mouse buttons (See page 8).
- Using the fill tool to add a coloured background.

Doing
- Click on the filled circle shape icon on the toolbar with the left mouse button, return to the screen and click on the colour black.
- Move on to the screen, position the cross that appears where you want to draw the cat's body. Click, let go and drag to get the size of circle you want. Click to keep the shape.
- Move the cross to a space above the body and drag out a smaller circle as before, for the head. It needs to touch the body. If you draw a shape that is the wrong size or in the wrong place click on the Undo tool on the toolbar and begin again.
- Click on the colour white with the left mouse button, move the cross on to the cat's body, click let go and drag out a white circle as its tummy. Click to keep the shape.

- Click on the filled triangle icon on the toolbar with the left mouse button, return to the screen, and click on the colour black. Move the cross to one side of the cat's head, click, let go and drag out a line to touch the cat's head, click, and drag out a triangle - it should be joined to the head. Click to keep the shape. Add a second ear in the same way on the other side of the cat's head.
- Go to the round brush icon on the toolbar, make the brush smaller, (about 30pt), using the left and right-hand mouse buttons (see page 8). Return to the screen, click on white, move to the cat's face and click to draw each eye in turn. Make the round brush smaller again (about 20 pt), click on green and click a smaller circle on each eye. Click on pink and click a nose. Make the brush smaller again, (about 15 pt), click on black and add a smaller circle to each eye and a curved row of dots for the tail.
- Reduce the round brush to its smallest (5 pt) and use it to draw whiskers.
- Click on the fill tool icon on the toolbar, return to the screen, click on red, click on the screen and the background to the cat will fill and become red.

Extending the Activity
- Draw a picture of two cats of different sizes and colours with a different coloured background.
- Combine filled shapes in other ways to draw an imaginary multi-coloured animal.
- Cut similar shapes out of coloured paper and make a collage picture of a cat or another type of animal.

Solid Shape Mouse

Tools to Use:

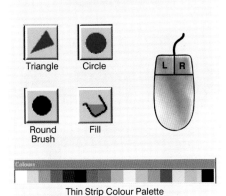

Triangle   Circle

Round Brush   Fill

Thin Strip Colour Palette

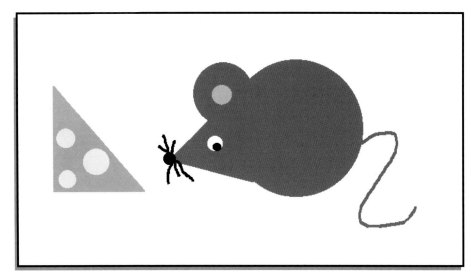

Talk About

- Drawing one shape, then drawing a second shape to join and touch it to make a new shape.
- Drawing shapes on top of other shapes using different colours.
- The shapes that need to be combined to make the shape of a mouse e.g. head, ears etc.
- Where to find these shapes and how to get them from the tool bar.
- Drawing these shapes in different sizes and colours.
- Reducing the size of the round brush using both the left and right-hand mouse buttons (see page 8).

Doing

- Click on the filled circle shape icon on the toolbar with the left mouse button, return to the screen and click on any shade of grey.
- Move to the screen, position the cross that appears where you want to draw the mouse's body. Click, let go and drag to get the size of circle you want. Click to keep the circle shape.
- Go to the filled triangle icon on the tool bar, click with the left mouse button, return to the screen, click a little way in front of the circle you drew and drag a line to join the circle. Click to end the line, then drag the line out to draw a triangle for the mouse's head. Click to keep the shape. This shape needs to be joined on to the body. If it does not, click on the Undo button on the toolbar and try again.
- Go to the filled circle icon on the tool bar, click with the left mouse button, return to the screen, position the cross that appears just above the body, close to where the head joins on, click and drag out a small circle to become an ear. This needs to be joined to the head. If it does not, use the Undo button as before.

- Go to the round brush icon on the toolbar, use the left and right mouse buttons to reduce the size of the brush to 30 pt (see page 8). Click on Close, return to the screen, click on the colour pink, go to the middle of the mouse's ear and click to add a pink inside to it.
- Reduce the size of the round brush to 20 pt, click on white, go on to the mouse's head and click to draw an eye, click on black with the same size brush, move to the point at the front of the head and click to draw a nose.
- Reduce the size of the round brush to 15 pt, move on to the white circle that is the eye, click near the bottom of it to add a pupil.
- Now reduce the size of the round brush to 5 pt and use it to draw black whiskers joined on to and coming out from the nose. Use the same size brush to click on the colour grey and draw a tail on the back of the body.
- Click on the filled triangle shape on the toolbar with the left mouse button, go to the colour orange click and then move to the screen. Click and drag out a line to start the shape of the cheese, click to keep the length of the line then click, let go and drag to draw a filled orange triangle. Click to finish and keep the shape
- Use the round brush, reduced in size, and the colour yellow to click circles as the holes in the cheese.

Extending the Activity

- Draw a different coloured mouse facing in the opposite direction.
- Draw two mice and a piece of cheese.
- Cut similar shapes out of coloured paper and make a collage picture of a mouse or another type of animal.

23

Aliens and Robots

Tools to Use:

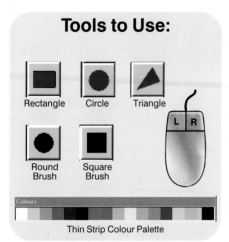

Thin Strip Colour Palette

Talk About

- Drawing one shape, then drawing a second shape to join and touch it to make a new shape.
- Drawing shapes on top of other shapes using different colours.
- The shapes observed on the faces of Aliens and Robots and how these are arranged and combined.
- Sketching some Alien and Robot faces in pencil on paper to explore ways of combining these shapes.
- Where to find these shapes and how to get them from the toolbar.
- Drawing these shapes in different sizes and colours.
- Reducing the size of the round and square brush using both the left and right mouse buttons (see page 8).

Doing

- Practise finding and drawing the large and small filled shapes that match those you have drawn.
- Practise reducing the size of the square brush and drawing lines and squares of different sizes.
- Practise reducing the size of the round brush and drawing circles of different sizes.
- Try putting different colour combinations together to get ones that you feel are appropriate for an Alien or Robot.
- When your ideas are complete you will want a clear screen to start your drawing. To do this click on the Dustbin icon on the toolbar with the left mouse button. The words 'Throw Away' and 'Cancel' will

appear. Click on Throw Away with the left mouse button and the screen will clear.

- First click on the filled shape icon you want for your Alien or Robot's head on the toolbar then return to the screen and click on the colour you want to use. Move back to the screen. Position the cross that appears where you want to draw the head. Click, let go and drag out the shape. Click to finish and keep the shape.
- You now need to add to this shape to make it into an Alien or Robot. Use different tools, different colours, different shapes and lines of different sizes in your drawing. Remember you can change the size of each brush by using the left and right mouse buttons (see page 8).
- Consider how many ears, eyes, antennae, aerials etc. it might have, what colours they are going to be, what size they are going to be and how they are going to be arranged on the head.
- Then your Alien or Robot will need; mouth, teeth, nose, cheeks, a neck and possibly shoulders too.
- Remember you can use the Undo tool on the toolbar to get rid of the last thing you drew if you do not want to keep it.

Extending the Activity

- Draw two similar Aliens or Robots on the screen but use different colours for each one.
- Draw two different Aliens or Robots on the screen but use the same colours for each one.
- Make a collage picture of an alien or robot using a range of different coloured papers and foil.

Exploring Fonts

Tools to Use:

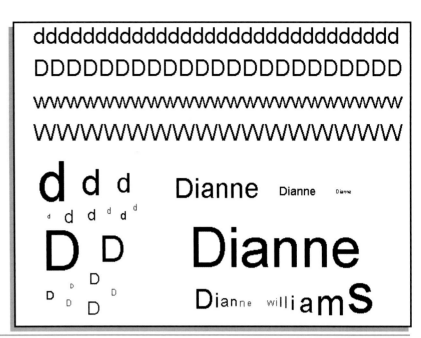

Talk About

- What the word 'text' means and which is the text tool on the tool bar.
- Cutting a collection of letters of different sizes out of newspapers and magazines.
- That each letter size has a number e.g. the text you are reading is size 11 pt.
- The size of the letters typed on the computer can be made larger and smaller by using the left and right mouse buttons.
- The cursor that appears on the screen needs positioning before starting to type words or sentences.
- The cursor needs removing before printing or the last letters typed will not print.
- Removing the cursor by clicking on the text tool with the left mouse button.
- Typing the same letter in several different sizes.
- Using the 'shift' key to get capital letters.

Doing

- Click on the text tool with the left mouse button, return to the screen, position the cursor where you want to type letters, click and type a row of letters from your name. Click to finish typing and keep the row of letters.
- Move the cursor to another part of the screen and click, you are now ready to begin typing further letters. This time hold down the 'shift' key on the keyboard whilst you type and your letters will now be capital letters. Click to finish typing.
- Move the cursor to another part of the screen, click and begin typing another row of letters. This time make some of your letters capital letters and some lower case.
- Go back to the text tool on the tool bar and click on it with the right mouse button. A window will appear with several labels on it. Look at the right -hand side of the window where it says 'size', there is a small box at the top with a number in it and a row of numbers in a box underneath. Next to the row of numbers are arrows and a bar to slide up and down. The up arrow will make the numbers in the box decrease in size and is used to make letters smaller. The down arrow will make the numbers in the box increase in size and is used to make letters larger. The bar can slide up and down and will do both.
- Click on a number in the box with the left-hand mouse button, the number you have clicked on will now be highlighted in blue. It will also appear in the 'size' box at the top of the window. Further down the window is a box with the word 'Sample' above it. The letters in this box will change in size to match the 'Size' number you chose - this is so that you can view your choice and change your mind if you want to by clicking on another 'Size' number.
- Try clicking on other numbers and watch the 'Sample' box change.
- To keep a letter size to type with on the screen, click on OK at the top of the window on the right-hand side, with the left mouse button, this will take you back to the screen. Position the cursor, click and begin typing letters in a new letter size. Click to finish.
- Try typing one letter from your name in several different sizes first in lower case letters and then in capitals.

Extending the Activity

- Type your Christian name in several different sizes using both capital and lower case letters.
- Type your Christian name making each letter smaller than the one before.
- Type your surname making each letter larger than the one before.
- Make a collage of one of the letters in your name by collecting lots of sizes and styles of text from newspapers and magazines.
- Make a collage of your name using letters of different sizes cut from newspapers and magazines.

Fonts and Colours

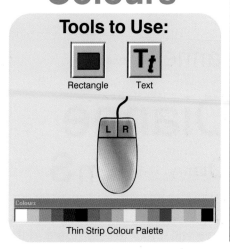

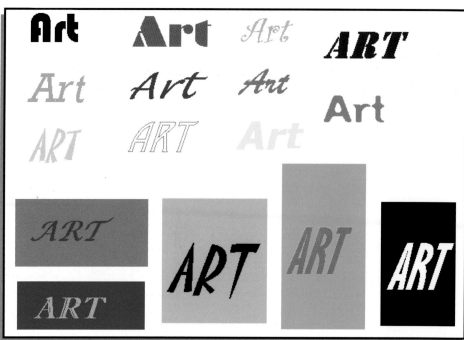

Talk About

- Which is the text tool on the tool bar and what the word 'font' means.
- Cutting a collection of different letter styles (fonts) out of newspapers and magazines.
- That different styles of letters (fonts) have different names e.g. Helvetica, Arial, Curlz etc.
- That it is possible to get and use lots of different fonts using the text tool and the left and right mouse buttons.
- The letters can be typed as capitals (using the shift key) as well as lower case in each font. The size of the letters can be changed as explored previously.
- Using different colours for each font.
- Removing the cursor by clicking on the text tool with the left mouse button.
- That the cursor needs positioning before beginning to type words or sentences and that it needs removing before printing or the last letters typed will not print.

Doing

- Click on the text tool on the toolbar with the right mouse button. A window will appear with several labels on it. Look at the top left-hand side of the window where it says 'Font ', there is a small box which will have the name of a font in it, and a list of lots of other fonts in a box underneath. Next to the list of fonts are arrows and a bar to slide up and down. The arrows are used to move up and down the list of fonts in order to choose one - the bar will move both up and down. When you choose a font and click on it with the left mouse button it will be highlighted in blue. It's name will appear in the small box at the top of the window and examples of the style of letters chosen will appear in 'Sample' box in the middle of the window. This means you

can view the style of letters and change your mind by clicking on the name of a different font if you don't like your choice.
- Try clicking on several different fonts and watch the 'Sample' box change.
- To keep a font style to type with on the screen, click on OK at the top of the window on the right. This will take you back to the screen, now position the cursor, click and begin typing. If you want letters in a different colour click on a new colour before you click and begin typing. The letters will now appear in the new colour.
- Try typing the same word e.g. Art, several times using a different font and a different colour each time. If you want to make the letters quite large, change their size, as you did previously, using the left and right mouse buttons before selecting different fonts.

Extending the Activity

- Go to the filled shape rectangle and click, return to the screen, click on a colour, position the cross that appears, click, let go and drag out a filled square or rectangle. Go to the text tool, use the left and right mouse buttons to choose a type and size of font. Return to the screen, click on a colour (different from the colour of the rectangle) position the cursor on the filled shape and type a word to fit on that shape. You may need to change the size or style of your font if the letters won't fit the first time.
- Draw several filled squares/rectangles in different sizes and colours. Type the same word e.g. Art on each one. Use a different font and a different colour each time - and make sure the letters fit on the shape!
- Cut squares and rectangles out of coloured paper and use text from newspapers and magazines to fit the same word in different styles on each one.

Section 2: Building on the Basics (for Lower Key Stage 2 pupils)

Teacher's Notes

In this section you will be using the suggested 'Lower Key Stage 2 Toolbar' combined with the 'Thin Strip Colour Palette' **for sessions 1 and 2 only**. The 'Simple Colour Palette' will be required from Session 3 onwards.

For this section you will need to make sure that the following tools are available on the toolbar.

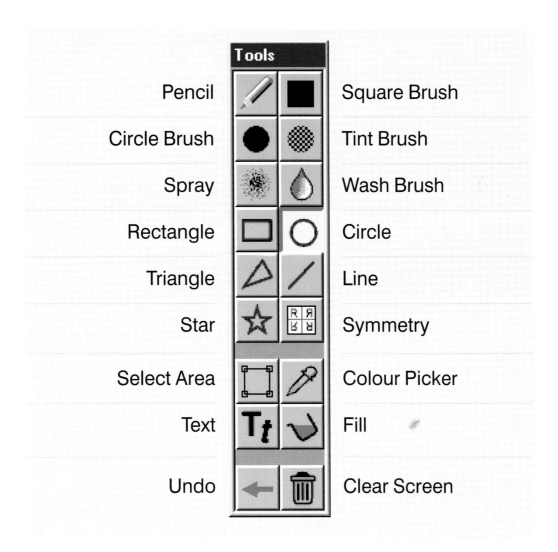

How to Construct the 'Lower Key Stage 2 Toolbar'

- The programme Dazzle should be open on the screen.
- At the top left hand side of the screen you will see the word Customize.
- Using the left hand mouse button click on the word customize and a drop down menu will appear.
- From the drop down menu click on the words Custom files and a box will appear on the screen.
- From this box, using the left hand mouse button, click on the word Dazzle. (If the word cannot be seen, you may need to use the small black down arrow to scroll up and down until the word is found.)
- Click on the button to the right of the menu labelled load.
- The full Dazzle Tool Bar (as shown on page 28) will now appear on the screen.

The Full Dazzle Toolbar

Tools

Pencil			Square Brush
Round Brush			Tint Brush
Diffuser Brush			Spray
Wash Brush			Stamp
Polygon			Star
Rectangle			Parallelogram
Triangle			Circle
Radial Lines			Line
Select Area			Colour Picker
Text			Fill
Show Grid			Zoom
Rainbow			Symmetry
Undo			Clear Screen

Customizing the toolbar by deleting tools

Deleting the tools from the toolbar is very simple.
• Hold down the key labelled Alt on the keyboard.
• At the same time, move your mouse pointer to the tool, which you want to remove.
• Keeping your finger pressed on the left hand mouse button, drag the tool to the centre of the
   drawing area (anywhere!) and release the mouse button.
• The tool will have been removed from the toolbar.
• You can create your new toolbar by deleting tools and saving it using the instructions below.

To create the suggested 'Lower K.S.2 Toolbar' remove the following from the Full Dazzle Toolbar.
• Diffuser brush
• Stamp
• Polygon
• Parallelogram
• Radial lines
• Show grid
• Zoom
• Rainbow

Saving the customized toolbar

Having created your new customized toolbar you can save it.
• Click on the word Customize from the top left corner of the screen.
• From the drop down menu, select custom files.
• Drag the mouse pointer over the name of the file in the box to highlight (in blue) this name, press the
   delete key on your keyboard to delete the name of the toolbar.

Don't panic! You have not deleted anything from the program; you have simply made a space to type in a name for the toolbar you have just created!

• In the empty box type in an appropriate name for your newly created toolbar e.g. Lower K.S. 2 Tools .
• Click on the Save button. Your toolbar will now be saved in the toolbar list.

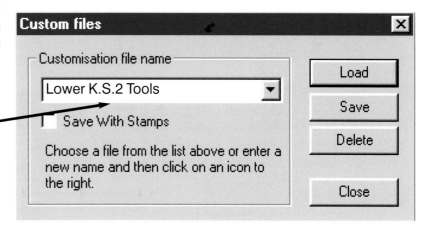

To use your new toolbar
• Go back to Customize at the top of the screen.
• From the drop down menu select custom files.
• Select the name of your new toolbar from the list.
• Click on the load button to load the toolbar ready for use.

The Simple Colour Palette

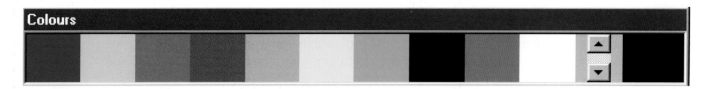

How to select the Simple Colour Palette

- Click on the word **Customize** from the top left corner of the screen.
- From the drop down menu, select **colours.** The following window will appear.
- Click on the small black downward pointing arrow and a drop down menu will appear showing you a choice of different palettes.
- Click on the name of the palette you wish to use e.g. **Simple Palette**. The Simple Palette will appear on your screen.
- Left click on the blue area above the palette and drag it to a convenient working position.

WHAT DO YOU ALSO NEED TO KNOW?

Where to find Move, Copy, Tile and Tile Flip

This is a super facility to produce stunning results in minutes.
- Using the select area tool, select a picture or part of a picture by dragging out a square shape over the top of the image you want to repeat (Example 1).
- From the top left hand corner of the screen select menu.
- You have several options to choose from this menu.
- Click on tile to see the image you selected, repeated all over the screen. Tile and flip will produce some mirror images (See example 2). Move, copy and stamp will allow you to move the mouse pointer to any are of the screen, press the mouse button and the new image will appear.

See also 'What do you also need to know?' on page 4

Example 1

Example 2

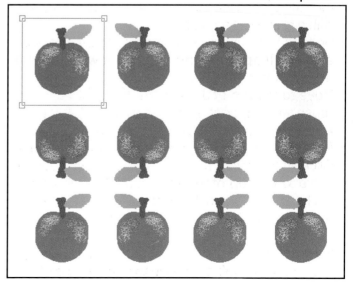

Building on the Basics 1
Colour Mixing
(Thin Strip Palette)

Tools to Use:

Round Brush

Thin Strip Colour Palette

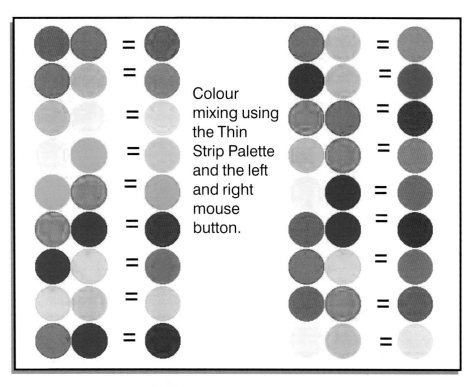

Colour mixing using the Thin Strip Palette and the left and right mouse button.

Talk About
- The tool that is going to be used and where it is on the toolbar.
- How to select the Thin Strip Palette (see page 4).
- Naming the colours on the Thin Strip Palette.
- Which is the left-hand mouse button and which is the right-hand button.
- Using the left-hand button first and then the right-hand button.
- Where the new colour that has been mixed will appear i.e. in the square at the end of the thin strip palette.

Doing
- Make sure the thin strip palette is on the screen.
- Click on the round brush icon on the tool bar with the left mouse button. Move to the screen, a circle with a brush will appear.
- Go to the colour brown on the thin strip palette, an arrow will appear, and click on it with the left mouse button.
- Move to the top of the screen, the circle and the brush will reappear, and then click the left mouse button. You will now have a filled brown circle.
- Return to the thin strip palette, an arrow will appear. Click on the colour red with the left mouse button.
- Move to the top of the screen next to the brown circle, the circle and the brush will re-appear. Click the left mouse button. You will now have a filled red circle.
- Return to the thin strip palette, click on the colour brown with the left mouse button and then click on

the colour red with the right mouse button. A new 'mixed' colour will appear in the box at the end of the thin strip palette.
- You do not need to click on this new colour, just return to the screen and move to the top in line with the other two circles. Leave a gap before clicking the left mouse button to add a filled circle of the new colour. You can draw in = in this gap with a pencil later after you have printed your work.
- Repeat the same sequence as you move along the thin strip palette until you have combined each adjacent pair of colours on the palette.
- Arrange the circles in a similar way as before but under the previous ones.
- Draw in = with a pencil after the work has been printed.
- Give each of the new colours that you have made a name.

Extending the Activity
- Mix colours together that are not next to each other on the thin strip palette. Click to draw filled circles in the colours you choose in the same way as before plus of course a circle in each new colour. Give each of the new colours a name.
- Combine white with each of the colours in turn.
- Combine black with each of the colours in turn.
- Combine a grey with each of the colours in turn.
- The children could explore colour mixing in a similar way by combining similar colours of paint.

Squares and Rectangles

Tools to Use:

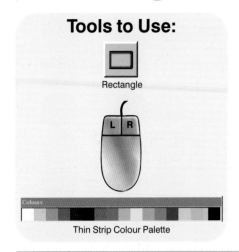

Rectangle

L | R

Colours

Thin Strip Colour Palette

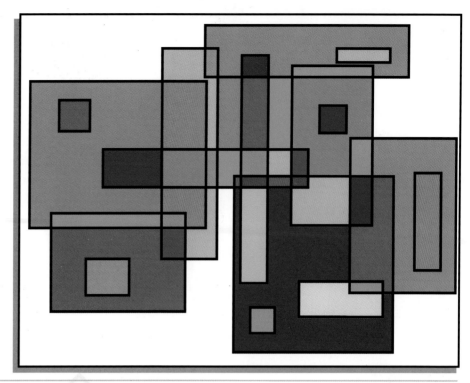

Talk About

- The tools to use and where they are found on the tool bar.
- What is special about a square shape and how it differs from a rectangle.
- How to fill and how to undo a fill.
- How to colour mix using the Thin Strip Palette and the left and right mouse buttons.

Doing

- Make sure the Thin Strip Palette is on the screen.
- Click on the rectangle icon on the tool bar with the left mouse button.
- Return to the screen, a cross will appear. Click on black with the left mouse button on the colour palette.
- Now position the cross where you want to draw your first shape. Click, let go and drag out a square or rectangle of any size. You can drag the shape out upwards, downwards or sideways. (It will always appear in red as you draw no matter what colour is chosen from the colour palette.) Click to keep the shape once it has reached the size you want. It will now revert to the colour chosen from the colour palette.
- Move to another part of the screen, position the cross where you want to draw your next square or rectangle. Click the left mouse button, let go and drag as before to draw a second shape. Make this shape a different size from the one before.
- Continue following this sequence until you have drawn lots of squares and rectangles of different sizes. Allow the shapes to touch and overlap and draw some shapes inside other shapes.
- Mix a new colour on the Thin Strip Palette using the left and right mouse buttons as directed on the previous page. Go to the fill tool and click on it with the left mouse button. Return to the screen. Place the arrow that appears inside one of the squares or rectangles you have drawn and click. The shape should now fill with the colour you have mixed. If you touch one of the lines that outlines a shape by mistake the whole drawing will change to the new colour; click on the Undo tool to get back to the original. Similarly if you click on the area outside the drawing by mistake that will fill with colour. Use the undo tool in the same way to rectify this.
- Continue mixing colours and filling each shape until all the drawing has been filled - all the colours used should be new colours which you have made and not the colours on the original Thin Strip Palette.

Extending the Activity

- Fill a set of squares and rectangles with colours you have made by adding black to each colour on the Thin Strip Palette.
- Fill a set of squares and rectangles with colours you have made by adding white to each colour in turn on the thin strip palette.
- Fill a set of squares and rectangles with colours you have made by adding a grey to each colour in turn on the Thin Strip Palette
- Paint an abstract picture made up of squares and rectangles. Fill each one with colours you have mixed.
- Make a collage of squares and rectangles using a range of coloured papers. Match these colours in paint (some of them will need to be mixed) and add further squares and rectangles to fill the paper.

Lighter and Darker

Tools to Use:

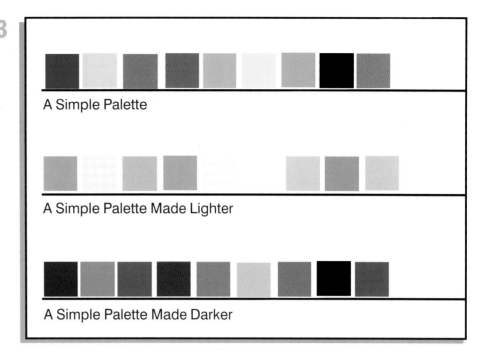

Square Brush

Simple Colour Palette

A Simple Palette

A Simple Palette Made Lighter

A Simple Palette Made Darker

Talk About

- How to select the Simple Colour Palette (see page 30).
- The colours on the Simple Colour Palette.
- The purpose of the two arrows at the end of the palette (i.e. making chosen colours lighter or darker - see below).
- Where each new colour will appear (i.e. in the square at the end of the simple palette.)
- How to return to an original colour (see below).
- Where the square brush icon is on the tool bar.

Doing

- Click on the square brush icon on the tool bar with the left mouse button.
- Return to the screen, a square with a brush will appear. Move down to the first shade of blue on the simple palette - an arrow will replace the square with a brush - and click on it with the left mouse button.
- Move to the top of the screen and click. A filled blue square should appear.
- Repeat this sequence with each of the colours on the palette. You should eventually have a row of filled squares in different colours.
- Now click on the first shade of blue on the simple palette with the left mouse button again. Next, click on the up arrow at the end of the simple palette several times with the left mouse button - the blue in the box should get slightly paler with each click. When you have a pale blue colour, move to the top of the screen until you are under the first blue square and click the left mouse button. A filled pale blue square should appear.
- Repeat this sequence with each of the colours on the palette. You should eventually have a row of filled squares in different pale colours.

- Click again on the first blue on the simple palette with the left mouse button. Now click on the down arrow at the end of the palette several times with the left mouse button - the blue box should get slightly darker with each click. When you have a dark blue colour, move to the top of the screen until you are under the pale blue square and click the left mouse button. A filled dark blue square should appear.
- Repeat this sequence with each of the colours on the palette. You should eventually have a row of filled squares in different dark colours.
- To return to an original colour, click on a colour on the simple palette with the left mouse button and the square at the end will change to match it.

Extending the Activity

- Make a row of squares with a dark and a light version of each colour in it.
- Make a row of squares that alternate dark then light in a mixture of colours.
- Make a row of circles that are dark at one end and light at the other.
- Use the left and right mouse buttons to colour mix using the simple palette in the same way as you did with the thin strip palette.
- Make each of these mixed colours lighter using the up arrow at the end of the palette. Print a row of circles using a pale version of each mixed colour.
- Make each of these mixed colours darker using the down arrow at the end of the palette. Print a row of squares using a dark version of each mixed colour.
- Mix primary colours with white and paint a picture or pattern in pale colours.
- Mix primary colours with black and paint a picture or pattern in dark colours.

Triangles and Circles

Tools to Use:

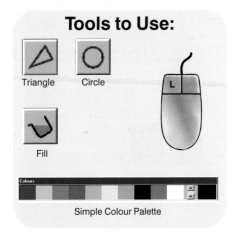

Triangle   Circle

Fill

Simple Colour Palette

Talk About
- The tools to use and where they are found on the toolbar.
- How to make colours on the Simple Palette lighter.
- How to make colours on the Simple Palette darker.
- How to return to the original colours.
- How to fill and how to undo a fill.

Doing
- Click on the triangle icon on the tool bar with the left mouse button.
- Return to the screen, a cross will appear. Position it where you want to draw your first triangle. Click the left mouse button, let go and drag out the red line that appears to the length that you want. Click to end the line - it will now disappear. Next, move the mouse and the outline (in red) of a triangle will take shape. Click the left mouse button to keep the shape when it is the size you want.
- Now move the cross to another part of the screen close to the first triangle and repeat the sequence to draw a second triangle. Make this one larger or smaller than the first one.
- Continue drawing triangles until you have a group of different sizes that touch, overlap and have smaller versions inside the larger ones.
- Click on a colour on the Simple Colour Palette with the left mouse button. Click several times on the down arrow with the left mouse button to make the colour in the end box darker. When you have a dark shade you like, go to the fill tool on the tool bar, click the left mouse button, return to the screen and position the arrow that appears inside one of the triangles, click and the shape will fill with the dark shade. Use this shade of colour to fill

several triangles before returning to the palette to make another colour darker in the same way and using it to fill further triangles.
- Continue making dark shades of each colour and using them to fill until all the triangles have been filled.
- If you have touched one of the lines whilst filling and the whole drawing has changed colour, click on the undo tool to rectify it. If you don't like a fill you have made you can get rid of it in the same way.
- Now use the circle tool to make a pattern of overlapping circles. Fill these shapes with lighter shades of the given colours using the arrow tool on the palette.
- Undo any mistakes using the undo tool as described earlier.

Extending the Activity
- Draw a group of triangles and fill them with a mixture of light and dark colours.
- Draw a group of circles and fill them with light and dark colours.
- Draw a group of both triangles and circles together and fill them with light and dark colours.
- Use the left and right mouse buttons as described on page 31 to colour mix and use the new colours to fill a group of circles and triangles.
- Add a very little black to different colours of paint and paint a dark pattern.
- Add a little of different colours of paint in turn to white and paint a pale pattern.
- Paint a pattern that uses both light and dark shades of different colours.

Tools to Use:

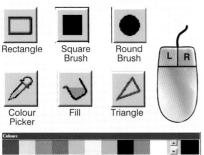

Rectangle Square Brush Round Brush

Colour Picker Fill Triangle

L R

Colours

Simple Colour Palette

Talk About

- The shapes, colours and patterns on the dress and in the background of the Gustav Klimt painting 'Portrait of Adele Bloch - Bauer I' - most are circles, squares and triangles in shades of brown, yellow, orange and gold.
- Where these shapes are found on the tool bar.
- The colours to use for a pattern and where they are on the Simple Palette.
- How to fill and how to undo a fill.
- How to get a colour you have mixed back again using the colour picker.
- How to make the round brush and the square brush smaller.
- Attempting just one pattern on a page.

Doing

- Choose two shapes e.g. rectangles and circles to use in a pattern.
- Click on black on the Simple Palette with the mouse button.
- Draw squares and rectangles of different sizes using the rectangle tool. (This is similar to using the triangle tool - see page 34) Draw some of them around the small ones and inside the larger ones. Arrange the shapes close to one another.
- Add some small filled squares by clicking on the square brush icon with the right mouse button to make the brush smaller, using the arrow down to about 18 pt, before clicking the left mouse button on close, returning to the screen, positioning the square and brush that appears where a filled square is wanted and clicking the left mouse button to add a square.
- Add some filled black circles to the inside of some of your shapes by using the round brush icon (using the same process as above).
- Go to the simple palette and click on yellow, orange or brown with the left mouse button. Select the fill tool, return to the screen and position the arrow that appears inside one of the squares or rectangles, click the left mouse button and the shape should fill with that colour.
- Use the same colour to fill more than one shape before following the same sequence with another colour.
- Use the up and down arrows at the end of the palette to make each colour i.e. yellow, orange and brown lighter and darker in turn by clicking on them with the left mouse button and use these new shades to fill other shapes.
- If you want to get back a colour you mixed previously to use again, click on the colour picker icon with the left mouse button. Return to the screen and position the colour picker icon on the colour in your drawing that you want to get back. Click on it with the left mouse button and that colour will appear in the box at the end of the simple palette. Click on it with the left mouse button and it is ready to use.
- Use the undo tool to rectify or change any fills you don't want.
- Choose a shade to fill the screen surrounding the shapes once they have all been filled.
- A second 'Klimt Style' pattern using triangles and circles can be drawn in a similar way.

Extending the Activity

- Draw a similar pattern using the same colours but combining all the shapes i.e. squares, circles and triangles.
- Design a new pattern of your own filled with the same Klimt colours.
- Change the colours in your pattern by filling over the top of the existing colours with a new group of colours - the colours could be from a different picture by Gustav Klimt.
- Make a collage pattern using the same shapes and colours and a range of different papers e.g. foil, tissue poster paper etc.
- Print a Klimt Style pattern using lids, boxes, strips of card, cotton wool buds etc. Mix, match and use the same colours in paint that can be seen in the original picture.

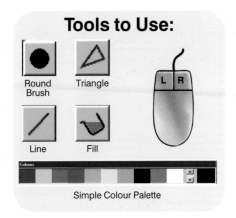

Tools to Use:

Round Brush

Triangle

L R

Line

Fill

Simple Colour Palette

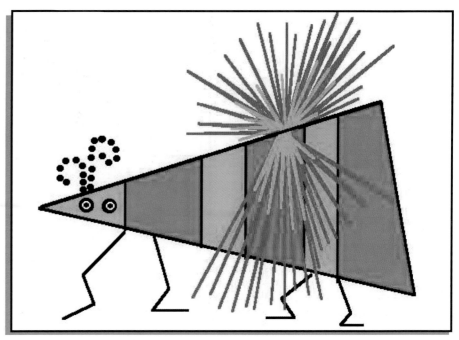

Talk About
- What makes a mini-beast- i.e. a body, legs, feelers, eyes and possibly wings.
- The line tool - where it is found and how to use it (see below).
- How to fill and how to undo a fill.
- How to make the round brush smaller by using the left and right mouse buttons.

Doing
- Click on the colour black on the Simple Palette with the left mouse button.
- Now click on the triangle icon on the tool bar with the left mouse button and return to the screen.
- Create a large triangle similar to the above example. (see page 34 for how to use the triangle tool.)
- Go to the line tool on the tool bar and click on it with the left mouse button. Return to the screen, position the cross that appears on one side of the triangle, click the left mouse button and drag a line across the triangle to the opposite side. Click the left mouse button to end the line and use the right-hand button to detach it.
- Continue drawing further lines until you have divided the triangle into a series of stripes.
- Use the line tool to add legs under the body.
- Go to the fill tool and click on it with the left mouse button, return to the Simple Palette and click on the colour green with the left mouse button. Move to your mini-beast and position the arrow that appears inside one of the stripes, click the left mouse button and the stripe should fill with green. If more than the stripe goes green the line you drew to make the stripe may not touch both sides of the triangle. Use the undo tool to return to the original and then re-draw the line.

- Fill each alternate stripe green and the others yellow.
- Reduce the round brush to 20 pt to do the black on the eyes 16 pt for the whites of the eyes and then to 7 pt to do the feelers and the inside of the eyes.
- Click on green with the left mouse button, click on the line tool with the left mouse button, return to the screen and position the cross on the top of the mini-beasts body towards the back. Click the left mouse button, drag a line upwards, click to stop, remain on the same line click to continue drawing and drag the line back to the mini-beasts body, click to stop and then click to start another line dragged out from the same point. Continue drawing lines in the same way both upwards and downwards from the same point.
- Click the right mouse button to stop drawing. Go to yellow on the colour palette, click the left mouse button before returning to the line tool. Click on it with the left mouse button and return to the screen to draw yellow lines on top of the green ones following the sequence described previously.

Extending the Activity
- Draw a similar mini-beast but in different colours.
- Draw a different mini-beast using different shapes but the same colours.
- Draw a different mini-beast using different shapes and different colours.
- Make a mini-beast in collage using a range of papers.
- Make a 3D mini-beast using reclaimed materials.
- Print a mini-beast using boxes, lids, cotton wool buds and strips of card.

Drawing a Dragonfly

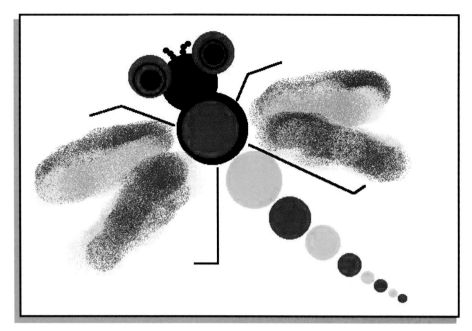

Tools to Use:

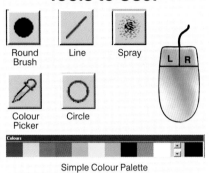

Round Brush | Line | Spray

Colour Picker | Circle

L | R

Colours

Simple Colour Palette

Talk About
- Pictures of dragonflies, the shape of their bodies, eyes, wings etc.
- How to colour-mix using the left and right-hand mouse buttons (see page 8).
- How to make colours lighter and darker using the up and down arrows at the end of the Simple Palette.
- How to make the round brush larger and smaller using the left and right mouse buttons.

Doing
- Click on the round brush icon with the right mouse button and make the brush larger, about 100 pt.
- Click on the colour black on the palette with the left mouse button and then move the circle and brush icon that appears to the part of the screen where you want to start the dragonfly's body. Click the left mouse button and a filled black circle should appear,
- Return to the round brush icon and use the right hand mouse button to reduce the size of the round brush to about 80 pt.
- Use this to add a smaller black circle above and joined on to the previous one, as the head.
- Keep the brush this size but use the left and right mouse buttons to colour mix red and blue on the Simple Palette to make purple. (see page 31)
- Use this colour to add a filled circle inside the black body shape.
- Reduce the size of the round brush to about 60 pt and add a purple filled circle either side of the head as the start of the eyes.
- Reduce the size of the round brush to about 25 pt, click on black on the palette and then add a black filled circle inside each purple eye.
- Reduce the size of the round brush to 5 pt and add two rows of dots as feelers in the middle of the top of the head.
- Use the circle tool to drag out a black circle to surround each filled black circle.
- Mix the colour purple and then make it paler by

clicking on the up arrow at the end of the palette with the left mouse button.
- Change the size of the round brush to 80 pt, return to the screen, click on the pale colour and add a filled circle of it under the black one that starts the body.
- Return to the palette and mix purple again, return to the tool bar, reduce the size of the round brush to about 40 pt, click on the colour purple, and add a smaller filled purple circle under the pale one.
- Keep using the same two colours alternately as you add filled circles to complete the body. Remember you can get a mixed colour back by clicking on the colour picker (see page 35).
- Reduce the size of the small brush each time as you add further filled circles and work down the body.
- Go to the spray gun, click on it with the left mouse button and then click on the colour you want to use on the Simple Palette. Return to the screen and spray a line of this colour to make part of the two wings on either side of the body.
- Click on another colour on the palette and add a sprayed line next to and touching the previous sprayed line.
- Build up the wings by adding further colour some of which you may have mixed.
- Add zig-zag legs to your dragonfly using the line tool (see page 36).

Extending the Activity
- Draw a similar dragonfly but use different colours e.g. green and blue.
- Draw a different sort of flying insect with a square head and eyes and a long body made up of different sized squares.
- Make a collage of a dragonfly using a range of different papers.
- Print a dragonfly using lids, boxes, cotton wool buds and strips of card.

The Tint Brush

Tools to Use:

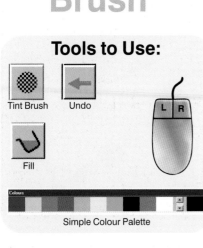

Tint Brush Undo

Fill

L R

Simple Colour Palette

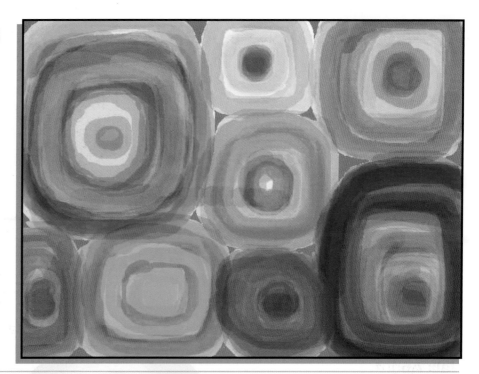

Talk About

- The tint brush - where it is found and how to use it (see below).
- The pale shade of colour that the tint brush will give when it is used initially.
- How the colour will deepen if the same colour is used on top of the first one.
- How colours will mix to make new colours if the new colour used for drawing overlaps the original one.
- How to use the undo tool to rectify work and return to the original. Remember you can only undo one move!
- The colours and shapes in the Kandinsky picture 'Colour study: Squares with Concentric Circles' and how they are arranged.

Doing

- Click on the tint brush with the right mouse button and reduce the size of the brush to 30 pt.
- Click on close with the left mouse button, return to the screen, a brush and a circle will appear. Move to the Simple Palette and click on the colour you want to use with the left mouse button before returning to the screen.
- Position the circle and brush that appears where you want to draw the centre of your first circle.
- Click and draw a filled circular shape. The colour will be very pale to begin with and you may want to draw on top of the same shape several times to get a deeper shade. Clicking the left mouse button to stop and then clicking it again and continuing over drawing in the same colour will also deepen the colour.
- Click the left mouse button on a second colour, return to the screen and add a ring around the centre of your circle. Allow this new colour to touch and overlap the first one in places, the colours will mix and new ones will appear.

- Continue using new colours and further rings until you have made a large circle of different overlapping colours.
- If you get a colour mix you don't like you can rectify it by clicking on the undo tool.
- As you are working in the 'Style of Kandinsky' and not trying to copy his work exactly, add further circles to your work following the same sequence. Use a range of different colours for each circle and make your circles different sizes randomly arranged on the screen rather than in rows of similar sizes as in the Kandinsky picture.
- Continue until the screen is full.
- There may be some small gaps around the edge of the screen and between some of the circles. To fill them, click on the fill tool with the left mouse button, return to the screen and click on the colour grey on the Simple Palette. Move back to the screen and position the arrow that appears in the gap that you want to fill and click the left mouse button. This gap should now fill with grey.
- Use the undo tool if you make any mistakes.

Extending the Activity

- Mix and make a new colour each time using the left and right mouse buttons on the Simple Palette when drawing a similar design of circles.
- Draw a similar design but use only the colours red and blue, make them lighter and darker using the up and down arrows at the end of the tool bar as well as mixing these two colours together.
- Draw a design that uses squares instead of circles.
- Mix pale shades of paint and paint a similar design of circles.
- Use only primary colours to paint a similar design.
- Mix secondary colours - orange, green and purple - and paint a similar design.

Different Stars

Tools to Use:

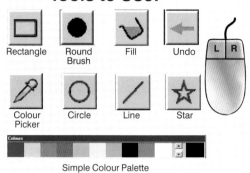

Rectangle Round Brush Fill Undo

Colour Picker Circle Line Star

Simple Colour Palette

Talk About
- Different sorts of houses and homes, the shapes observed on different sorts of buildings and how those shapes fit together.
- The star tool and how to use it (see below).
- How to fill and how to use the undo tool to rectify a mistake

Doing
- Select the line tool. Left click on the left hand side of your screen and drag a line across your page. Left click again to finish this line and then right click to disconnect. In this way draw three lines across the bottom of your page. Each line needs to touch both sides of the screen or else when the gaps between them are filled the colour will flood other parts of the picture.
- Click on the rectangle icon and drag out the shape of each house or block of flats in turn. Use the same tool to draw smaller shapes as windows and doors.
- Reduce the size of the round brush to 5 pt and use it to add a door knob to each door by clicking the left mouse button.
- Add lines across the windows using the line tool.
- Draw the shape of the roofs using the line tool, clicking to start, clicking to stop, then clicking to change direction as you have done previously.
- Draw the porch over the door of the flats in the same way.
- Colour each building grey and each window yellow using the fill tool (see page 34).
- Make the grey on the Simple Palette slightly darker using the down arrow at the end of the palette. Use this dark grey to fill the doors.
- Make the turquoise on the Simple Palette darker in the same way and use it to fill the sky around the houses.

- Fill the bottom stripe across the screen with black and the one above it with green.
- Go to the star icon on the tool bar, click on it with the left mouse button and return to the screen. Click on the colour white on the Simple Palette with the left mouse button, move on to the screen and position the cross on the part of the sky where you want to draw the first star. Click the left mouse button, let go and drag out a star shape to the size you want. Click the left mouse button, to keep the star. Add several more stars in the same way. All these stars will have 5 points.
- Change the number of points the next group of stars have by clicking on the star icon with the right mouse button, change the number 5 that appears in the box to 8 by clicking on the up arrow with the left mouse button then clicking on close, returning to the screen and adding more stars in the same way as before - all these stars will have eight points.
- Change the number of points on the next group of stars you draw to 12 following the same sequence and finally draw some stars with 16 points in the same way.

Extending the Activity
- Draw a row of houses that are similar, but fill each one with a different colour. Add a star to match the colour of each house.
- Draw a group of houses surrounded by stars in different colours and with different numbers of points.
- Draw an imaginary house of the future using different shapes and colours surrounded by a group of stars.
- Make observational drawings of houses and homes in the locality.
- Make an observational drawing of your own house.

Tiling Text

Tools to Use:

Tt
Text Tool

Select Area Tool

Fill Tool

L R

Colours

Simple Colour Palette

+ Use the **Area** menu on the top tool bar

Dianne Dianne Dianne Dianne D
Dianne Dianne Dianne Dianne D
Dianne Dianne Dianne Dianne D
Dianne Dianne Dianne Dianne D
Dianne Dianne Dianne Dianne D
Dianne Dianne Dianne Dianne D
Dianne Dianne Dianne Dianne D
Dianne Dianne Dianne Dianne D
Dianne Dianne Dianne Dianne D
Dianne Dianne Dianne Dianne D

Talk About
- How to change the size and style of fonts (see below).
- What the select area tool looks like and where it is found.
- Where the Area menu is on the top tool bar.
- What the word 'tile' means.
- How to fill.

Doing
- Click on the text tool with the right mouse button. Look at the list of fonts on the left-hand side of the box that appears. Use the left mouse button to move the bar in the strip at the side of the box between the up and down arrows, downwards until you see the font you want to use - this one is Bauhaus 93- click on it to highlight it with the left mouse button. It is now ready to use.
- Change the size of the font by moving the bar in the strip between the up and down arrows in the box labelled 'Size' down to the size required - this one is 36pt - click on it to highlight it with the left mouse button. It is now ready to use.
- Position the cursor that appears where you want to type your name. It will automatically be in black unless you have selected another colour.
- Type your name once then click two spaces using the space bar before typing your name again.
- Go the fill tool and click on it with the left mouse button, return to the screen and click on the colour red on the Simple Palette with the left mouse button. Move back to the screen and position the arrow that appears on each of the letters in the second version of your name in turn, click the left mouse button each time and they will change to red.

- Now click on the select area tool on the tool bar with the left mouse button and return to the screen. Position the cross that appears close to, and just above, the first version of your name.
- Click the left mouse button, hold it down and drag out a box to surround both of your coloured names, the box will be red in colour. Don't click again or the box will disappear. There is a small square in each corner of your box, if you click on any of these small squares with the left mouse button you can move the sides of the box inwards or outwards. Make sure it is as close to the words as possible.
- Move the arrow that appears as you move away from the box to the word 'Area' on the top tool bar, click the left mouse button and a menu of options will appear. Move down to the word 'Tile' and it will become highlighted in blue. Click the left mouse button and the two versions of your name will now tile to form a repeating pattern in red and black all over the screen.
- Click the left mouse button outside of the select area box to remove it, if it is still on the screen.

Extending the Activity
- Follow the same sequence but use a different font and different colours.
- Follow the same sequence but use a different font for each name as well as a different colour.
- Follow the same sequence but type three versions of your name and then tile them.
- Print a repeating pattern using a design made from draught excluder stuck on an aerosol lid. Alternate the colours used as in you did on the computer.

Tile and Flip

Tools to Use:

+ Use the **Area** menu on the top tool bar

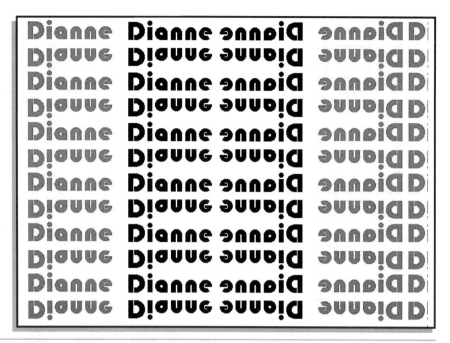

Talk About

- How to change the size and style of a font (see page 40).
- The select area tool and how to use it (see page 40).
- The difference between tiling an image and tiling and flipping an image (i.e. some of the images will be the right way up, others will be upside down and back to front.)
- How to fill.

Doing

- Click on the text tool with the right mouse button and following the sequence described on page 40, change the size and style of the font. The one used here is Bauhaus 93 size 36.
- Click on OK with the left mouse button, return to the screen and position the cursor that appears where you want to type the first version of your name. Check the palette colour used is black.
- Type your name once then click two spaces using the space bar before typing your name again.
- Go to the fill tool and click on it with the left mouse button, return to the screen and click on the colour red on the Simple Palette with the left mouse button. Move back to the screen and position the arrow that appears on each of the letters in the second version of your name in turn, click the left mouse button each time and they will change to red.
- Now click on the select area tool on the tool bar with the left mouse button and return to the screen. Position the cross that appears close to and just above the first version of your name.
- Click the left mouse button, hold it down and drag out a box to surround both of your coloured names. The box will be red in colour.

- There is a small square in each corner of your box, if you click on any of these small squares with the left mouse button you can move the sides of the box inwards or outwards to make sure it is as close to the words as possible.
- To keep the box, don't click but move the arrow that appears as you move away from the box to the word 'Area' on the top tool bar. Click the left mouse button and a strip of options will appear. Move down to the words 'Tile and Flip' and they will become highlighted in blue.
- Click the left mouse button and the two versions of your name will form a repeat pattern that fills the screen. Some of the names will be the correct way up but because others have been flipped the letters in some cases will be back to front or upside down - or both!
- Click the left mouse button with the cursor outside the selected area to get rid of the select area box if it is still on the screen.

Extending the Activity

- Follow the same sequence but use different fonts and different colours.
- Follow the same sequence but use a different font for each name as well as a different colour.
- Follow the same sequence but type three versions of your name before tiling and flipping them.
- Draw a design on a press print tile, ink it up and print one row in which the design is upright and a second row where the design has been flipped and is upside down.
- Print a repeating pattern using a design made from draught excluder stuck on an aerosol lid. Alternate the colours in the first row where the design is upright and in the second row as well where the design has been flipped and is upside down.

Roman Tiles

Tools to Use:

Square Brush · Round Brush · Fill · Rectangle · Undo · Select Area

Simple Colour Palette

+ Use the **Area** menu on the top tool bar

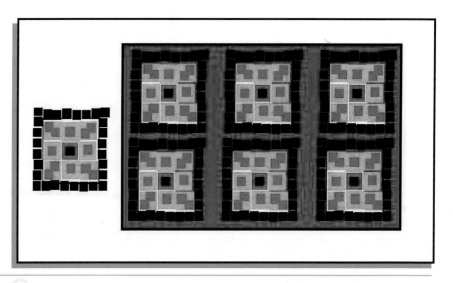

Talk About
• The sorts of colours to use for a Roman mosaic.
• How to make colours lighter and darker using the Simple Palette (see page 33).
• How to reduce the size of the square brush (see page 35).
• How to get and use the select area tool.
• How to rectify a mistake using the undo tool.
• How to find 'Tile' using the 'Area' menu on the top tool bar.

Doing
• Go to the rectangle icon on the tool bar and click on it with the left mouse button.
• Return to the screen and position the cross that appears where you want to draw your square shape. Click the left mouse button, let go and drag out a square to the size you want. Click the left mouse button to keep the shape.
• You are going to work on and inside this square to create your Roman mosaic design for tiling.
• The square brush will need reducing in size to about 15 pt using the left and right mouse buttons as you have done before. Click on Close with the left mouse button to return to the screen.
• Click on the colour you want to use on the Simple Palette with the left mouse button. Move the brush icon that appears inside the square that you have drawn.
• By continually clicking the left mouse button you will be able to create a design of small filled squares inside this initial square.
• Go to the Simple Palette and click on new colours with the left mouse button as you add to your design.
• Remember you can make colours lighter and darker and use those too by clicking on the up and down arrows at the end of the Simple Palette.

• The tiles need a border of squares around the outer edge of the original drawn square.
• When your tile design is complete, go to the select area tool on the tool bar and click on it with the left mouse button.
• Return to the screen and position the cross that appears close to your tile, click the left mouse button and drag out a box to surround your tile. Use the small squares in the corners of the box to drag it in as close as possible to the edges of your tile.
• Don't click but move the arrow that appears as you move away from the box to the word 'Area' on the top tool bar and click the left mouse button. A menu of options will appear. Move down to the word 'Tile', which will become highlighted in blue. Click the left mouse button and the screen will fill with a repeated pattern of your design.
• If there are gaps between the tiles select a colour from the Simple Palette by clicking on it with the left mouse button then click on the fill tool, return to the screen and position the arrow that appears in each gap in turn. Click the left mouse button and they will fill with colour.

Extending the Activity
• Draw a new and different Roman mosaic design using a different group of colours.
• Use a circle instead of a square as the starting point for a tile in an Aboriginal style.
• Make a Roman mosaic design using cut paper squares or impressing objects into a square clay tile to make a pattern.
• Print an Aboriginal design using round lids and cotton wool buds and paint.

Building on the Basics 13
Symmetry

Tools to Use:

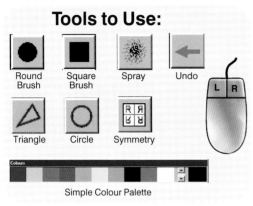

Round Brush | Square Brush | Spray | Undo

Triangle | Circle | Symmetry

Colours

Simple Colour Palette

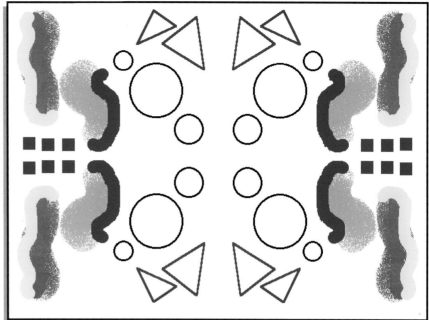

Talk About
- What the word 'symmetry' means.
- What the symmetry tool looks like and where it is found.
- How to draw circles and triangles of different sizes (see page 34).
- How to make the round brush and the square brush smaller using the left and right mouse buttons.
- How to change colours and how to rectify a mistake.

Doing
- Click on the symmetry tool on the tool bar with the left mouse button - (It looks like a square divided into four with an 'R' in each quarter.)
- The screen will now be divided into four quarters by two red lines that cross over in the middle.
- You are only going to work in one of these quarters. Whatever you draw in one quarter, will appear in the other three as well.
- Click on the circle icon on the tool bar with the left mouse button. Return to the quarter of the screen you are going to work in and position the cross that appears where you want to draw a circle. Click the left mouse button, let go and drag out a circle shape. Click the left mouse button again to keep the shape when it is the required size. Identical circles should now be in each quarter of the screen.
- Add further circles of different sizes in the same way but only draw in one of the quarters on the screen.
- In a similar manner, use the triangle tool to make

triangles of different sizes in the same quarter of the screen (see page 34).
- Go to the spray gun icon and click on it with the left mouse button. Return to the screen, click on the colour you want to use from the Simple Palette with the left mouse button. Move to the quarter of the screen you used before and add some sprayed lines. Change colours for each line. Identical coloured lines will appear in each quarter of the screen.
- Go to the round brush icon, reduce the size of the brush to 15 pt using the left and right mouse buttons and return to the screen. Click on a colour on the Simple Palette and draw some lines in the quarter of the screen you used before. Add further lines in different colours. Identical lines will appear in each quarter on the screen.
- Use the square brush tool in a similar manner.
- When your pattern is finished, remove the red symmetrical lines by clicking on the symmetry tool with the left mouse button.

Extending the Activity
- Draw a different symmetrical design using lines only but using lots of different colours.
- Draw a different symmetrical design using shapes only but using lots of different colours.
- Divide a piece of paper into four and print an identical design in each quarter using lids, boxes and cotton wool buds.
- Paint a pattern using the same colours in identical parts of each quarter of the paper so that they match.

Stars

Tools to Use:

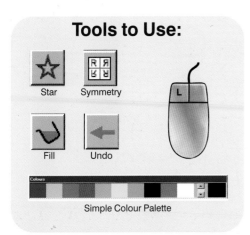

Star Symmetry

Fill Undo

Simple Colour Palette

Talk About
• Using different shades of two colours to fill the drawing - in this case blue and turquoise.
• How to make a colour lighter and darker using the up and down arrows at the end of the Simple Palette.
• Where to start drawing each time - (in the centre of the screen where the lines of symmetry form a cross.)
• How to use the undo tool to rectify a mistake.

Doing
• Click on the symmetry tool with the left mouse button. Two red lines will appear on the screen and form a cross.
• Click on the star icon on the tool bar with the left mouse button and return to the screen.
• Position the cross that appears exactly in the centre of the screen where the two lines cross over. Click the left mouse button, let go and drag out a large star shape. It will appear to have many points and part of it will be in each quarter of the screen because you are using the symmetry tool. You are in fact only using the standard star with 5 points. Click the left mouse button to keep the star when it is the size you want.
• Position the cross exactly back in the centre of the screen where the lines cross, click the left mouse button, let go and drag out a smaller star inside the first one. Click the left mouse button to keep the star when it is the size you want.
• Position the cross again in the centre of the screen, click the left mouse button, let go and drag out a smaller star inside the last one you drew. All the stars will appear to have many points that cross over because you are using the symmetry tool.
• Click on the fill tool on the tool bar with the left mouse button, return to the screen and click on blue on the Simple Palette with the left mouse button. Move the arrow that appears on to the

screen and position it inside one of the points on one of the stars. Click the left mouse button and this point will fill with blue as will the identical points of this same star in the other quarters of the screen.
• Repeat above using turquoise.
• To fill the rest of the points and shapes inside the stars use the same two colours - blue and turquoise - but change the shade of each one using the up and down arrows at the end of the Simple Palette.
• Remember you can undo a fill by clicking on the undo tool with the left mouse button. You will only be able to undo the last fill you made.
• Click on the symmetry tool with the left mouse button when you have completed your fill.
• This activity would link to looking at Islamic designs and patterns.

Extending the Activity
• Draw a similar design but fill it with two different colours and lighter and darker shades of those colours.
• Draw a similar design but fill it with colours you have mixed using the left and right mouse buttons on the thin strip palette (see page 31).
• Draw a similar design but remove the symmetry tool by clicking on the tool bar with the left mouse button. Now, when you use the fill tool, you won't get a symmetrical fill. Fill each part of each star with a different colour.
• Cut a large star out of coloured paper and decorate it with shapes cut out of other papers in different shades of blue. Use identical shapes on the same part of each point.
• Draw a star design on squared paper, colour it in different shades of blue.
• Use identical colours on the same part of each point.

Drawing a Butterfly

Tools to Use:

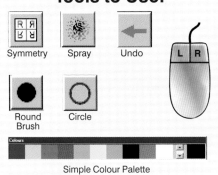

Symmetry Spray Undo

Round Brush Circle

Simple Colour Palette

Talk About

- How to change the lines of symmetry i.e. click on the symmetry tool on the tool bar with the right mouse button. A box labelled 'Symmetry' will appear. Inside the box are three options. Click on the tick next to left/right symmetry with the left mouse button. Click on OK with the left mouse button and the red line for left/right symmetry will appear on the screen.

Doing

- Follow the sequence described above.
- Select the spray gun and the colour red. Position the circle and brush ready to draw. (You only need to work on one half of the screen, the line of symmetry will automatically make the shape you draw appear on the other half of the screen as well.) Click the left mouse button and draw a large wing at the top and a smaller wing at the bottom. Spray inside each wing to add some colour.
- Select the round brush icon and place a red filled circle inside the middle of the bottom wing.
- Next, increase the size of the round brush to 90 pt and add a large filled red circle inside the middle of the top wing.
- Select the circle icon and drag out a ring to surround the large filled circle. Draw a circle in the same way around the smaller filled circle inside the bottom wing.
- Reduce the size of the round brush to 50 pt and add a filled white circle inside the red filled circle on the top wing.
- Click on the colour red and use the up arrow at the end of the palette to make the colour paler and pinker. Reduce the size of the round brush to 20 pt and add a pink circle inside the filled circles on both wings.
- Click on the circle icon and drag out a pink ring to surround the top pink circle.
- Using the round brush at size 15 pt, add filled black dots in the middle of the circles on both the top and

bottom wings. Add rows of dots following the shape of the outer edge of each wing.
- Keep the same brush size but click on the colour white and add a row of white dots close to and following the outer edge of each wing. Reduce the round brush to 10 pt, click on the colour red and add a red dot to the middle of each of the white dots.
- Return to the symmetry tool and click on it with the left mouse button to remove the lines of symmetry in order to add the body.
- Select the round brush at size 70 pt and add a filled black circle as the butterfly's head.
- Reduce the size of the round brush to 50 pt, click on the colour red and add a row of filled red circles down the length of the butterfly as the body. Make some of the circles smaller as you get towards the end.
- Reduce the size of the round brush to 40 pt, click on the colour black and add filled black circles inside the red ones down the length of the body. Reduce the size of these as you get towards the end.
- Restore the lines of left/right symmetry, reduce the size of the round brush to 6 pt and add a row of black dots as a feeler to one side of the head. It will automatically appear on the other side as well.

Extending the Activity

- Draw another butterfly in the same way but use different colours and decorate it differently.
- Draw another butterfly using left/right symmetry but use a different range of tools.
- Make a symmetrical print by folding a piece of paper in half, putting paint down the centre fold, refolding the paper and pressing both sides together working from the centre outwards.

45

Teddy Bear

Tools to Use:

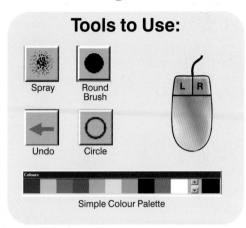

Spray

Round Brush

Undo

Circle

L R

Colours

Simple Colour Palette

Talk About
- How to reduce the size of the round brush using the left and right mouse buttons. (see page 8)
- How to make a colour lighter using the up arrow at the end of the Simple Palette.
- How to rectify a mistake using the undo tool.

Doing
- Select the spray gun tool. Return to the screen and click on the colour brown with the left mouse button.
- Position the circle and brush that appears in the centre of the screen, click the left mouse button, hold it down and drag the mouse in a circle to draw the body of the bear. Draw inside the circle as well to add colour. To deepen the colour draw over the shape several times. Let go of the mouse to stop drawing.
- Drag the mouse in a similar way to draw a smaller circle as the head at the top of, and joining on to the body. Again, draw inside this shape and over the top of it to deepen the colour.
- Draw two small circles as ears on either side of the head in the same way.
- Drag out a spray gun line for each of the bear's arms and legs. Add a small circle as a paw at the end of each one, still using the spray gun.
- Go back to the Simple Palette and make the colour brown paler by clicking on the up arrow at the end of the Simple Palette with the left mouse button. Add a little of this pale colour to the centre of the head using the spray gun.

- Using the circle tool and the colour brown, drag out a small ring inside each ear. Click the left mouse button to keep the ring.
- Select the round brush tool and reduce to size 20 pt. Select the colour black and make a black dot for the nose.
- Reduce the size of the round brush to 17 pt and add two eyes on either side of and just above the nose.
- Reduce the size of the round brush to 5 pt and use it to draw two curved lines under the nose as the mouth.
- Draw two lines on each of the paws at the end of the arms and three lines on the each of the paws at the end of the legs.
- Save your drawing on a disc to use for the next activity.

Extending the Activity
- Draw another teddy bear in a different colour e.g. yellow or black and white.
- Draw a teddy bear that is similar to one you own or that belongs to a friend.
- Draw a multi-coloured teddy bear.
- Make an observational drawing of a teddy bear. Try to convey its furry texture in your drawing by adding groups of lines in different directions.
- Make an observational painting of a teddy bear using a piece of sponge or a sponge brush to give the idea of texture. Add detail to your painting by drawing on it using oil pastel crayons when it is dry.

Many Bears

Tools to Use:

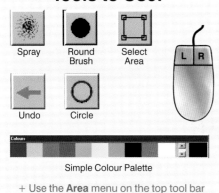

Spray   Round Brush   Select Area

Undo   Circle

Simple Colour Palette

+ Use the **Area** menu on the top tool bar

Talk About

- How to use the select area tool and how to extend or reduce the box it establishes around a drawing by using the small squares in the corners of the box.
- Where the 'Area' menu is on the top tool bar and how to use it.
- How to use the undo tool to rectify a mistake.
- Loading the image of the teddy bear if it has been saved on disk for use in this activity.

Doing

- Load the image of the teddy bear drawn in the previous session if it has been saved on a disk (see page 6) - or draw a teddy bear following the instructions given on page 46.
- Go to the select area tool, click on it with the left mouse button and return to the screen.
- Position the cross that appears as close as possible to the drawing of the bear at the top of it on the left-hand side. Click the left mouse button, hold it down and drag out a box around the teddy bear shape.
- If the box needs moving closer to or further away from the teddy bear, click on and use the little squares in the corner of the box to move the sides. Don't click to keep the box, just move to the word Area on the top tool bar and click on it with the left mouse button. Select the word 'Copy'.
- Return to the screen, a cross in a box will appear. Position this where you want another drawing of your teddy bear, click the left mouse button and a second version of your drawing will appear. Move the box with the arrows inside it to another part of the screen, click the left mouse button again

and a further version of your drawing will appear.
- If your original drawing of a teddy bear was in the middle of the screen it might be advisable to click and add the extra drawings at the edges of the screen. You may only be able to fit part of the area box on the screen in this case and then only part of the image will be copied - rather like a repeat pattern on a piece of wrapping paper.
- Points to remember - if the box with the arrows in it touches or covers part of a drawing already on the screen it will cover or hide part of that drawing when the left mouse button is clicked. You can rectify such mistakes by clicking on the undo tool with the left mouse button. This will undo all the copies you have made and you will need to start the whole sequence again from using the select area tool onwards.

Extending the Activity

- Make a new drawing of e.g. a flower, a house or a mini-beast. Print a copy of this single drawing and then a copy of your multiple drawings. You now have a design for a piece of wrapping paper and a matching card.
- Draw a design of multi-coloured squiggles that overlap and use these as a single unit for a card and multiple copies as wrapping paper.
- Look at shapes that repeat themselves in natural objects e.g. segments in a slice of orange, the dots on a sea-urchin, the spirals on a shell etc and use these as a stimulus for observational drawing.
- Look for and record shapes that repeat themselves in the built environment e.g. brick patterns, railings etc.

Building on the Basics 18
Licquorice Allsorts

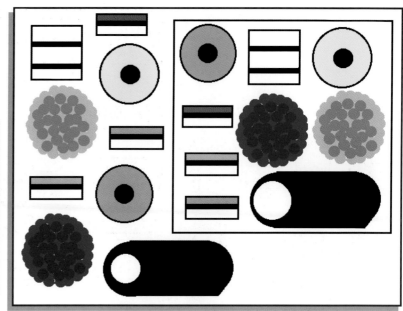

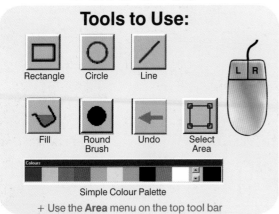
Talk About
- The tools on the tool bar that match the shapes of the Licquorice Allsorts.
- The colours on the Simple Palette that match those on the Licquorice Allsorts and those that will need to be mixed or made lighter or darker.
- How to rectify a mistake using the undo tool.
- How to use the select area tool to move objects (see below).

Doing
- Look at the different shapes of the Liquorice Allsorts and decide which and how many to draw. Nine Licquorice Allsorts in total have been drawn here, each filled with the colours that match the actual sweets.
- The square and rectangular ones have been drawn using the rectangle tool. They have been divided into stripes using the line tool and the stripes coloured using the fill tool. Orange was made by mixing red and yellow on the Simple Palette using the left and right mouse buttons. Brown was taken directly from the Simple Palette and the pink was made using red and making it paler by clicking on the up arrow at the end of the Simple Palette with the left mouse button.
- The round ones were drawn using the circle tool and then filled with colour. The centres of the sweets were made by clicking with the round brush reduced to 40 pt.
- The cylindrical black and white ones were drawn using the circle tool. Two circles of similar size were drawn slightly apart and then joined together using the line tool. The lines link the tops and bottoms of the circles to make a new shape. This was filled with black and the white circle at the end was added by clicking with the round brush size 50 pt.
- The knobbly sweets were drawn using the circle icon, to establish the outline, then filled by clicking with the round brush size 10 pt. Similar clicked circles were added around the outline. The pale

pink colour was mixed and blue was taken from the palette. Further clicked dots were added to the centre of these using the round brush size 15 pt in a darker shade of both pink and blue made by using the up and down arrow at the end of the palette.
- To group the Licquorice Allsorts closer together each of them will need to be moved individually. Go to the select area tool on the tool bar, click on it with the left mouse button, return to the screen and drag a box as close as possible around the sweet to be moved.
- Don't click (you will; loose the box if you do) but select the 'Area' menu on the top tool bar. Go down the list of options to select the word 'Move'. Return to the screen, the image of the sweet will have disappeared and instead a box will appear.
- Position this where you want the sweet to re-appear, click the left mouse button and the sweet will appear in a box with small squares in each corner. If the sweet is where you want it, click on the screen with the left mouse button and the box will disappear. Repeat the same sequence to move each sweet into the group. If a sweet is not where you want it e.g. if it is touching or overlapping another sweet and you want to re-position it, you can do so whilst it is still inside the box by selecting the word 'Move' in the 'Area' menu. Re-position the sweet, click the left mouse button and it will re-appear in its new position. Move each Liquorice Allsort in the same way until together they form a more compact group.
- Save the work on a disk (see page 6).

Extending the Activity
- Draw some triangles and stars of different sizes and move them together.
- Draw some stars, squares and circles and move them together to form a group.
- Make an observational drawing of a group of Licquorice Allsorts.
- Use boxes, lids and other reclaimed materials to make 3D Licquorice Allsorts. Paint them in the appropriate colours and arrange them in a group.

Licquorice Allsorts Tiled

Tools to Use:

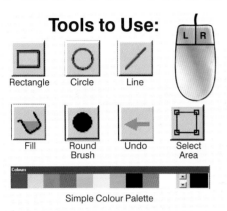

Rectangle Circle Line

Fill Round Brush Undo Select Area

Simple Colour Palette

+ Use the **Area** menu on the top tool bar

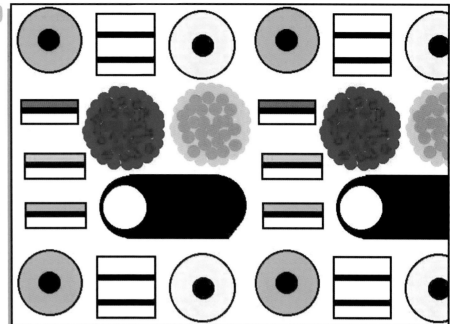

Talk About
- Loading the work if it has been saved on a disk. (see page 6).
- How to access 'Tile' and 'Tile and Flip' (see page 41).
- How to rectify a mistake or return to the original group of Licquorice Allsorts using the undo tool on the tool bar.

Doing
- If your image is already on a disk, load this onto the screen. If not, create a group of Licquorice Allsorts using the instructions on page 48.
- Go to the select area tool on the toolbar, click on it with the left mouse button and return to the screen.
- Position the cross that appears close to the top of the group of Licquorice Allsorts on the left-hand side.
- Click the left mouse button and drag out a box to surround the group of Licquorice Allsorts. Use the small squares in the corners of the box to drag the box in as close as possible. Don't click to keep the box, but select the word 'Area' on the top tool bar. Select the word 'Tile' which will become high-lighted in blue.
- Click the left mouse button and the screen will fill with a repeat pattern of your Licquorice Allsorts.

- If you want to keep this pattern save it on a disk.
- If you do not like this pattern, click on the undo tool with the left mouse button and the screen will clear, leaving only the original group of Licquorice Allsorts.
- Return to the word 'Area' on the top tool bar and select the words 'Tile and Flip'.
- Click on them with the left mouse button and the group of Licquorice Allsorts will now fill the screen as a different repeat pattern i.e. some of the sweets will be facing different directions.
- If you decide you like this pattern save it on a disc.

Extending the Activity
- Change the colours of the Licquorice Allsorts in your original group before you tile them.
- Change the colours of the Licquorice Allsorts in your original group again before tiling and flipping them.
- Print a repeat pattern using boxes, lids and cotton wool buds in the colours of the Licquorice Allsorts.
- Cut the shapes of Licquorice Allsorts out of different papers and arrange them as a repeat pattern.

Draw a Clown

Tools to Use:

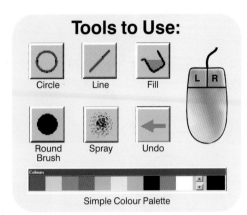

Circle   Line   Fill

Round Brush   Spray   Undo

L   R

Simple Colour Palette

Talk About
- What clowns look like, the clothes they wear, the way they paint their faces and what they wear on their heads.

Doing
- Use the circle tool to draw the face of the clown.
- Go to the Simple Palette and make pink by clicking on red and then continually clicking on the up arrow at the end of the Simple Palette with the left mouse button. Use the fill tool to fill the circle with pink.
- Select the line tool to drag and click several times to draw the outline shape of the clowns hat. Use the fill tool and black to colour the inside of the hat.
- Select the spray gun, mix orange using red and yellow with the right and left mouse buttons and use it to spray and add hair to the side and top of the clown's face.
- Select the round brush and reduce the size to 40 pt. Select red from the colour palette and add a filled circle as the clowns nose.
- Keep the brush the same size, click on the colour green and make it paler by clicking on the up arrow at the end of the palette. Use this pale green and the left mouse button to click and add four circles on the left-hand side of the clowns hat. Now mix purple using red and blue with the left and right mouse buttons and add four further circles inside the green leaves as a flower. Mix pink for the circle in the centre of the flower. Reduce the brush to15 pt, mix purple again and add another circle inside the pink one.
- Keep the brush at 15 pt, click on black and draw a cross for each eye. Click on white and with the same size brush click a circle in the middle of each cross. Reduce the brush to 10 pt, click on black, then add a small circle in the middle of the white ones.

- Mix orange and use the size 10 pt brush to click a row of circles as eyebrows over each eye.
- Increase the brush to 15 pt, mix a darker shade of pink than the colour of the face and click a circle either side of the face as cheeks.
- Increase the brush to 30 pt, click on red and draw a curved line on the face as the mouth. Reduce the brush to 15 pt, click on white and add a curved white line on top of the red one. Reduce the brush to 8 pt, click on black and add a black curved line on top of the white one to complete the mouth.
- Click on red and draw a line under the face to the outer edges of the screen on both sides as the shoulders of the clown. Use the fill tool and the colour red to fill this shape.
- Increase the size of the round brush to 40 pt, mix purple by clicking on red and blue using the left and right mouse buttons and click a row of circles as the collar under the face. Mix orange by clicking on red and yellow with the left and right mouse buttons. Add alternate orange circles between the purple ones on the collar.
- Reduce the size of the brush to 10 pt, mix a pale green and add a row of circles above and touching the previous row. Reduce the brush to 8 pt and add white dots on top of the green ones.
- Increase the size of the brush to 50 pt and add some large white circles to the clown's clothes. Reduce the brush to 35 pt and add some red circles inside the white ones. Finally mix purple, reduce the brush to15 pt and add purple circles inside the red ones.

Extending the Activity
- Draw a similar clown but use different colours.
- Draw a different sort of clown but use the same colours as in the activity.
- Make a clown's face on a paper plate using wool, card and different sorts of papers

Section 3: Extending the Ideas (for Upper K.S.2 pupils)

Teacher's Notes

In this section you will be using the 'Full Dazzle Toolbar' combined with the 'Full 216 Colour Palette' and, in Session 20, the '16 Grey Scale Palette'.

New tools for this section

Using the skills learned in the previous section (See pages 27-29), either use the 'Full Dazzle Toolbar', or create a custom 'Upper Key Stage 2' toolbar which contains the following tools, as well as those used in Lower K.S.2.

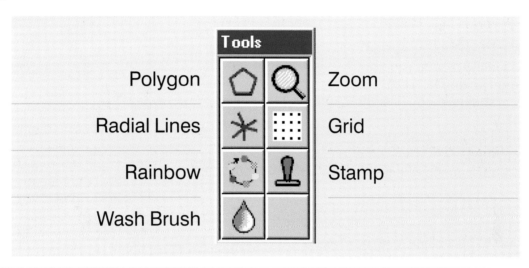

	Tools	
Polygon	⬠ 🔍	Zoom
Radial Lines	✳ ⣿	Grid
Rainbow	🔄 ⬱	Stamp
Wash Brush	💧	

Changing the palette to 216 colours and greyscale

In the previous section you learned how to change the colour palette to a Thin Strip (page 4) and the Simple Palette (page 30). Try changing the colour palette again and for this section you will need to use the 216 Colour Palette and the Grey Scale Palette.

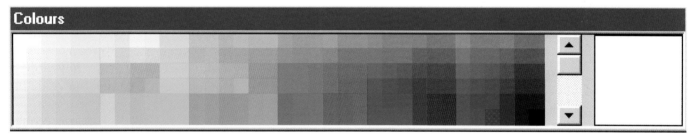

216 colour palette

Helpful hint

Sometimes the colour palette and the toolbar can take up space on the drawing area of the screen obscuring your image.

You can move them around on the screen. Using the mouse, point to the title bar at the top of the toolbar or palette, click with the left mouse button and drag the toolbar or palette to another part of the screen.

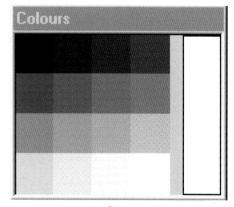

Grey scale palette

WHAT DO YOU ALSO NEED TO KNOW?

Where to find Scale, Flip X and Flip Y

You will already be familiar with some aspects of this section, which you applied when copying and repeating an image in section 2.

Example 1

- Using the select area tool, select the picture or part of the picture you want to scale or change (Example 1) by dragging out a square shape over the top of the image.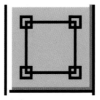
- From the top left hand corner of the screen select 'Area'.
- From the drop down menu select 'Scale'.
- Nothing appears to happen but…
- Using the select area tool, draw out a smaller square at the side of the other image (Example 2). This will appear to be a blank area, however, a copy of your image will appear but smaller.
- You can repeat the process making the image larger.

Example 2

Flip X and Flip Y

- You can also have fun flipping the image upside down. Select the menu button as above but try using the options Flip X and Flip Y (Example 3)

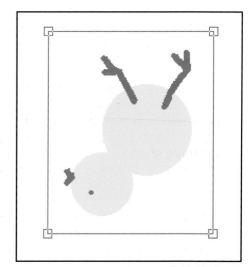
Example 3

See also 'What do you also need to know?' on pages 4 and 30

Extending the Ideas 1
Collecting Colour Families

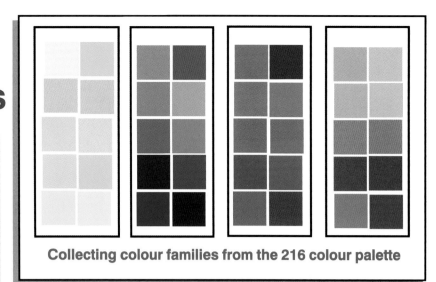

Collecting colour families from the 216 colour palette

Tools to Use:

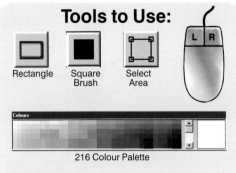

Rectangle Square Brush Select Area L R

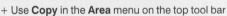

216 Colour Palette

+ Use **Copy** in the **Area** menu on the top tool bar

Talk About
- What a colour family is.
- The colour families on the 216 colour palette.
- How to use the rectangle icon.
- How to use the select area tool to outline a rectangle.
- How to find 'Copy' in the 'Area' menu.
- Using 'Copy' to repeat the rectangle shape several times.
- How to move the colour palette to different parts of the screen.

Doing
- Click on the rectangle icon with the left mouse button.
- Return to the screen, position the cross that appears where you want to draw a rectangle. Click the left mouse button, let go and drag out a tall, narrow rectangle shape. Click the left mouse button to keep the shape.
- Click on the select area tool with the left mouse button.
- Return to the screen, position the cross as close as possible to the top left-hand corner of the rectangle drawn previously. Click the left mouse button, let go and drag out a box to surround the rectangle shape
- Use the small boxes in the corners of the larger box to drag its edges as close as possible to the outline of the rectangle.
- Don't click (or you will loose the box) but move to the 'Area' menu on the top tool bar.
- Scroll down until the word 'copy' appears highlighted in blue.
- Return to the screen, an empty red rectangle will appear. Position it where you want a second rectangle, click the left mouse button and the outline of a second rectangle, that is a copy of the one drawn initially, will appear.
- Position the empty red rectangle where you want the third and then the fourth rectangle and click the left mouse button to copy them in the same way.

- Click on the square brush icon with the left mouse button, return to the screen and click on a shade of yellow on the colour palette with the left mouse button. Move the brush and square that appears to the inside of the first rectangle, click the left mouse button and a filled yellow square will appear.
- Return to the colour palette, click on a different shade of yellow, move back inside the rectangle and click the left mouse button to add another filled square of yellow.
- Continue selecting and adding further squares in different shades of yellow until the rectangle is full.
- Fill the second rectangle in the same way but select and use squares in different shades of blue.
- Fill the third rectangle with squares in different shades of red.
- Fill the final rectangle with squares of green.

Extending the Activity
- Make collections of other colour families in the same way e.g. pink or brown.
- The up and down arrows at the end of the colour palette when clicked on will make colours lighter and darker. Use the arrows and make a colour family in e.g. light greens and then a second colour family of dark greens.
- Reduce the size of the square brush to 30 pt, click and collect a small group of squares in different shades of blue, then red, then yellow, and finally green. Use the select area tool to draw a box around the combined colour groups, go to the 'Area' menu, select 'Tile' and click to fill the screen with a repeat pattern.
- Make a colour family in collage using magazine pictures.
- Mix two colours of paint, using different amounts of each to make a colour family - include black and white to lighten or darken some of the shades.

Extending the Ideas 2
The Willow Pattern

Tools to Use:

Round Brush | Spray | Fill

Line | Pencil | Undo | Polygon

Colours

216 Colour Palette

Talk About
- Look at and discuss the images on Willow Pattern plates or in books that illustrate the story.
- Make rough outline drawings in a sketchbook of images selected to use in a piece of work and how they might be combined.
- Where the blue colour family to be used for the work is found on the 216 colour palette.
- How to use the undo tool to rectify a mistake.
- How to reduce the size of the round brush using the left and right mouse buttons (see page 8).

Doing
- The images taken from the Willow Pattern illustrated here were drawn in the following way using a colour family of blues from the 216 colour palette.
- The shape of the pagoda on the bottom right-hand side was drawn using the rectangle icon, the line tool and the round brush clicked to add the windows. The roof was drawn using the polygon icon for the centre, the line tool to create triangles either side and the round brush clicked to add filled circles on the points. (N.B. The polygon is used in the same way as the triangle tool - see page 34.)
- The ground in front of the pagoda was drawn using the pencil and the round brush reduced to 20 pt.
- The tree behind the pagoda was drawn using the pencil, the circle icon and the round brush clicked to add filled circles.
- The pattern above the tree was drawn using the line tool.
- The boat was drawn using the round brush reduced to 5 pt and the line tool.
- The willow tree on the left-hand side was drawn using the round brush reduced to 10 pt and the spray gun.
- The ground around the tree was drawn using the pencil.

- The bridge was drawn using the round brush reduced to 10 pt.
- All the shapes were filled in different shades of blue chosen from the 216 colour palette. Remember that if one of the shapes you fill has an incomplete outline the whole screen will fill with colour. To rectify this click on the undo tool on the tool bar and over draw to add to and complete the outline of the shape before using the fill tool again.
- Try to find and use shades of blue that are similar to those used on Willow Pattern plate or in book illustrations of the story.
- Save your work on a disk and print it out.

Extending the Activity
- If you want to add further drawings to your picture, reload it from the disc, draw the extra lines and shapes you want or change some that you drew before, then save your work on the disk under a new file name. The original drawing will still be on the disk as well.
- Make a similar drawing using black and drawing only the outline of shapes rather than filling them in. Save this outline drawing on a disk. Reload it and fill it with a different colour family e.g. green. Save and print out your drawing. Reload the outline drawing again and this time, fill it with shades of red. Save and print out your drawing.
- Write comments about how your drawing appears when the different colours are used.
- Draw a design using the same tools as before and include different objects from the story.
- Mix a blue colour family using paint. Give each shade of blue a name of its own.
- Paint a picture of your own using this family of colours.
- Make a colour collection of different shades of blue using different papers, different drawing media and magazine pictures.

Drawing Picasso Style

Tools to Use:

Line · Fill · Undo

216 Colour Palette

Talk About

- Portraits painted by Picasso that are very angular and that depict features e.g. noses and eyes in strong, unusual shapes e.g. 'Weeping Woman' and portraits of 'Dora Maar'. Make sketches of the shapes of some of the different facial features in the portraits in a sketchbook.
- Look at, discuss and describe the type of colours Picasso used for these portraits. Name the colours and make a collection of them in a sketchbook using wax crayon or oil pastel.
- Where colours that are similar to these can be found on the 216 colour palette.
- How to use the line tool (see below).
- How to use the undo tool (see page 5).
- Adding lines and shapes to the background of the portrait that are similarly angular.

Doing

- Click on the line tool on the tool bar with the left mouse button, return to the screen, click on black on the colour palette with the left mouse button then move back to the screen and position the cross that appears where you want to start drawing. Click the left mouse button, let go and drag out a line. Click the left mouse button again to keep the line when it is the required length. After you have clicked you can continue drawing the line and change direction if you want. Click the right mouse button to stop drawing.
- Draw the outline of the head and shoulders first, then divide the head into different angular shapes.
- Once the face has been divided up the features i.e. nose, eyes, cheeks, mouth and teeth can be drawn using the line tool. Make these angular in shape as well.

- Add lines and shapes either side of the face as hair and a shape on top of the head as a hat.
- Divide up the area around the portrait into a series of shapes using the line tool. Some of these shapes need to be angular.
- Remember you can use the undo tool to rectify your drawing but it will only undo the last move you made.
- Click on the fill tool on the tool bar with the left mouse button, return to the screen and click on the colour you want to use from the colour palette with the left mouse button. Return to your drawing, position the arrow that appears inside the shape to be filled and click the left mouse button. The shape should now fill with colour. If other parts of the screen fill as well there must be some gaps in your drawing. Click on the undo tool, then select the line tool and add further drawing to the outline of the shape you tried to fill - before filling it again!
- Continue filling all the shapes both in the portrait and in the background. Make sure you choose and use similar strong colours like Picasso.
- Save your work on disk and print it out.

Extending the Activity

- If you have saved the drawing on disk you will be able to reload it, make changes to it or add additional drawing to it before saving it under a new file name and printing it out. The original drawing will still be on the disk as well.
- Draw a different Picasso style portrait and fill it with a different range of colours.
- Cut angular shapes out of different colours of paper and make a Picasso style collage portrait.
- Paint or draw a self-portrait or portrait of a friend in the style of Picasso.

Extending the Ideas 4
Scaling and Distorting

Tools to Use:

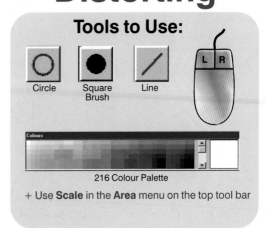

Circle | Square Brush | Line | L R

216 Colour Palette

+ Use **Scale** in the **Area** menu on the top tool bar

Talk About
- What the words 'Scale' and 'Distort' mean.
- Using the line tool (see page 55).
- How to reduce the size of the round brush (see page 8).
- How to find 'Scale' in the Area menu on the top tool bar (see page 52).
- How to use the undo tool to rectify a mistake (see page 5).

Doing
- Click on the circle icon on the tool bar with the left mouse button and return to the screen. Position the cross that appears where you want to draw a face. As you are going to draw several faces in different sizes it would be advisable to draw the first one on the left-hand side of the screen close to the top.
- Click the left mouse button, let go and drag out a circle shape to the size you require. Click the left mouse button to keep the shape.
- Use the circle icon again to draw the outline shapes of the eyes.
- Reduce the size of the round brush to about 30 pt using the left and right mouse buttons. Return to the screen, position the circle and brush that appear where you want the centre of each eye (in turn) click and a filled circle will appear each time.
- Move the circle and brush to the position of the mouth and click three circles that touch and overlap to create a surprised expression.
- Select the line tool to draw eyebrows above each eye and a straight line downwards between the eyes as a nose.
- Go to a pink on the 216 colour palette, click on it with the left mouse button, return to the screen and position the brush and circle where you want each

cheek (in turn) click and a filled pink circle will appear.
- Select the fill tool and the colour red. Move to the screen, click the left mouse button to fill around the face red.
- Click on the select area tool on the toolbar with the left mouse button, return to the screen and position the cross that appears close to the face on the top left hand side, click the left mouse button, let go and drag out a box around the face keeping as close to the outline as you can.
- Don't click or you will lose the box but go to 'Area' on the top tool bar, scroll down until you come to the word 'Scale', click the left mouse button and return to the screen.
- The original drawing will still be on the screen but the box around it will have disappeared. Hold down the left mouse button and drag out a new box - it can be any shape or size, tall, thin, large, small etc. Release the left mouse button and a copy of the original face will appear on the screen, this time it will match the size and shape of the new box you drew.
- Repeat this procedure drawing a different size box each time so that each face that appears will be distorted in a different way. Fill the screen with several distorted versions of the same face.

Extending the Activity
- Draw a different motif e.g. a house and explore distorting it.
- Use the text tool to type your name and explore distorting it.
- Make an observational drawing of e.g. a shoe. Distort these drawings using grids as shown in Step by Step Art Book 4.

Scaling and Tiling

Tools to Use:

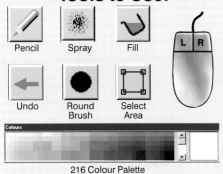

Pencil   Spray   Fill

Undo   Round Brush   Select Area

216 Colour Palette

+ Use **Copy** in the **Area** menu on the top tool bar

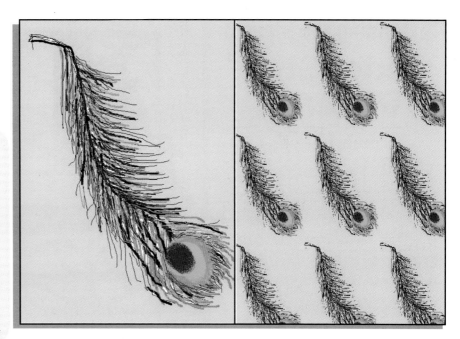

Talk About
• The colours on an actual peacock feather and where similar colours can be found on the 216 colour palette.
• The sort of lines and the arrangement of lines that make up a peacock feather and the tools that will draw similar lines on the tool bar.

Doing
• Select the fill tool, pick a light green from the colour palette and fill the screen.
• Click on the round brush and reduce its size to 10 pt using the left and right mouse buttons. Return to the screen, click on a dark blue on the 216 colour palette, go back to the screen and draw a long curved line as the central spine of the feather. Add some lines of the same thickness and colour on either side of the spine.
• Click on the spray gun icon on the toolbar with the left mouse button, return to the screen, click on a green on the 216 colour palette with the left mouse button. Go to the top of the spine of the feather, click the left mouse button and move round to spray a circle of green. Remember to deepen the colour you can spray over the same area several times.
• Now click on a different green on the colour palette with the left mouse button, return to the screen, click the left mouse button again and move round on top of the previous circle to spray a smaller circle in this second shade of green.
• Click on a dark blue on the 216 colour palette with the left mouse button, return to the screen, click the left mouse button again and move round on top of the previous circle to spray a small dark blue circle.
• Add lines on either side of the spine using the round brush size 10 pt and shades of blue and green.
• Finally add more lines in the same colours on

either side of the spine between and on top of the other lines using the pencil tool. These will be much thinner and will complete the drawing of the feather.
• To tile this feather it will first need to be scaled down. To do this click on the select area tool on the toolbar with the left mouse button. Return to the screen, position the cross that appears on the left-hand side of the screen near the top, click the left mouse button and drag out a box around the drawing of the feather.
• Don't click (or you will lose your box) but move to the 'Area' menu on the top tool bar, scroll down to the word 'Scale' click the left mouse button and return to a space on the screen either above or below the drawing of the feather. Hold down the left mouse button, drag out a small box and then let go. The feather drawing will appear reduced to the size of the small box. The original drawing will still be on the screen.
• Return to the select area tool on the tool bar and click on it with the left mouse button. Go to the screen, position the cross that appears close to the top left-hand corner of the small drawing of the feather. Click the left mouse button and drag out a box around this small drawing.
• Don't click but move to the 'Area' menu on the top tool bar and scroll down to the word 'Tile'. Click the left mouse button and the screen should fill with a repeat pattern of tiled peacock feathers.

Extending the Activity
• Scale and tile other on-screen drawings of linear objects e.g. dried grasses or cow parsley.
• Make an observational drawing on paper in biro of a piece of lace.
• Make a similar drawing, reduced in size, on a small tile of press print. Ink up the press print and on a new piece of paper print a repeat pattern using the tile several times.

Extending the Ideas 6
Tudor Style Patterns

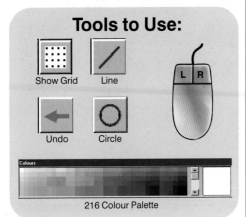
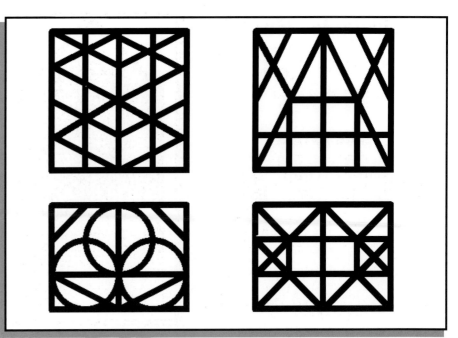

Talk About
- What the grid icon looks like and where it is found on the toolbar.
- How to get a grid on the screen (see below).
- How to get rid of the grid by clicking on the grid icon on the toolbar with the left mouse button.
- How to draw on the grid with the line tool.
- How to make a thicker line by clicking on the line tool on the toolbar with the right mouse button. A box with the words 'Line Width' will appear on the screen. Next to the box are two arrows, clicking on the up arrow with the left mouse button will make the line thicker and clicking on the down arrow with the left mouse button will make the line thinner. When the line is the desired width click on the word close at the bottom of the box with the left mouse button and return to the screen to draw lines of that width.
- The shapes and patterns seen in black and white on Tudor 'style' buildings. Posters, postcards and photographs will be necessary for this part of the activity.

Doing
- Make some rough sketches of simple Tudor style patterns in a sketchbook. Focus on patterns that are made up mainly of lines and circles as these are the tools that are going to be selected and used from the tool bar.
- Click on the grid icon on the toolbar with the left mouse button - the screen will now have a dotted grid all over it.
- Now click on the line tool on the toolbar with the right mouse button and then click on the up arrow with the left mouse button to increase the width of the line. Click on close with the left mouse button to keep the line when it has reached the required width.

- Make sure the colour black has been chosen from the 216 colour palette.
- Return to the screen and position the cross that appears on the dot on the grid where you want to start your drawing. Click the left mouse button and drag out the red line that appears. Click the left mouse button to end a line or to stop the line and change direction. Click the right button to cut off a line you have finished with.
- Try drawing lines diagonally from dot to dot as well as horizontally and vertically.
- Use the undo tool if you want to rectify a mistake - remember it will only undo the last move. If you want to rub out more see page 4.
- Click on the circle icon on the toolbar with the left mouse button, return to the screen, position the cross that appears on the dot where you want to start drawing, click the left mouse button and drag out a circle on the grid, click the left mouse button to keep the circle when it is the required size. Add further circles to the design if required. N.B. Because the thickness of the straight line has been altered, the circles will have thicker outlines as well.
- Save the designs on a disk before printing it out.

Extending the Activity
- Draw some Tudor style designs using the grid and very thin lines.
- Draw some Tudor style designs using the grid and a mixture of thick and thin lines.
- Select and tile one design filling the screen with a repeat pattern of a Tudor design.
- Use some thin strips of black paper and on squared white paper produce several collage patterns 'Tudor style'.

Extending the Ideas 7
Stained Glass Windows

Tools to Use:

Show Grid   Line   Fill

L R

Undo   Circle

Colours

216 Colour Palette

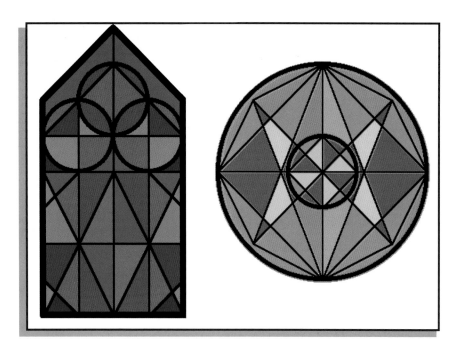

Talk About
- How to make the lines thicker and thinner using the left and right mouse buttons.
- How to select and how to remove the grid by clicking on the grid icon on the toolbar with the left mouse button.
- The shapes and colours found in stained glass windows - postcards, photographs and old Christmas cards will be needed as source material for this.

Doing
- Left click on the grid tool.
- Right click on the line tool and increase the width of the line by left clicking on the up arrow. Left click on close to keep the width of the line before returning to the screen to begin drawing.
- Position the cross that appears on a dot, click the left mouse button and drag out the red line to draw the outline shape of a stained glass window. Remember that to stop a line or to change direction of a line, click the left mouse button. Click the right mouse button to cut off a line.
- Once you have completed the outline reduce the width of the line, return to the screen and add some more lines inside the outline to divide the window shape into sections.
- Select the circle tool and add three circles to the design.

- Click on the grid tool to remove the grid. The fill tool will not operate if the grid is still on the screen.
- Select the fill tool and pick a colour you want to use from the palette. Fill some sections of the window with this colour. Use several different colours in turn to fill the other sections of the window.
- Draw a second stained glass window but make this one circular in shape.
- Save your work on disk before printing it out.

Extending the Activity
- Draw two window shapes similar to the previous ones and fill each window with the same range of colours.
- Draw two identical window shapes and fill each one with a different range of colours.
- Fold and cut a circle of black paper to remove a number of large shapes. Keep the outside border intact. Stick coloured tissue paper on the back of the cut out shapes to complete a collage stained glass window.
- Cover a sheet of white paper with a thick covering of different colours of wax crayon. Cut a black window silhouette as before and stick it on top of the colouring. Trim off any excess paper.

Extending the Ideas 8
Drawing Doors

Tools to Use:

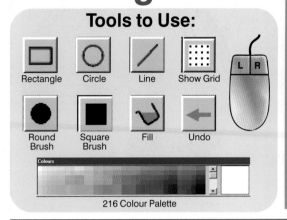

Rectangle Circle Line Show Grid

Round Brush Square Brush Fill Undo

Colours

216 Colour Palette

Talk About

• Using the square brush as a rubber (see page 4).
• How to rectify a mistake using the undo tool.
• How to get rid of the grid by clicking on the grid icon with the left mouse button.
• The shapes found on and around doors - pictures and postcards will be necessary as source material for this or alternatively observational drawings of doors in the locality.

Doing

• The example described here is the grey door on the blue background.
• Select the grid tool.
• Select the line tool and increase the line width (see page 58).
• Select the circle tool and drag out a large circle that almost touches the top of the screen. Click the left mouse button to keep the circle.
• Click on the line tool and draw a horizontal line across the upper part of the circle, extending a little on each side. Cut off with a right click.
• Click on the square brush icon with the left mouse button and then on the colour white on the palette and use the square brush as a rubber to remove the bottom half of the circle that is below the horizontal line. Click on black to continue drawing.
• Select the line tool and draw in the sides of the door frame.
• Right click on the line tool to make the line width smaller.
• Left click the grid tool to remove the grid from the screen.
• Select the line tool and draw a line across the bottom of the door frame. Add lines to draw a rectangular shape on either side of the door frame and to divide the semi-circle at the top of the door into shapes like a fan light.

• Select the rectangle tool and drag out a rectangle shape on the left hand side of the door near the top. Draw a similar shape on the right-hand side of the door again near the top.
• Draw two square shapes in the same way on either side near the bottom of the door.
• Draw smaller squares and smaller rectangles inside these shapes.
• Click on the round brush with the right mouse button and use the left mouse button to reduce the size of the brush to 30 pt.
• Return to the screen and use it to draw a letter box and door knob.
• Reduce the size of the round brush again to 10 pt and use it to draw a door knocker.
• Select the fill tool and then click on grey on the colour palette and move the arrow that appears on the screen to the shapes inside and on either side of the door. Click the left mouse button to fill them with grey.
• Click on black and use it to fill the smaller squares and rectangles on the door. Finally click on a blue and use it to fill the scene around the door.

Extending the Activity

• Look at the example of the door on the red background and try and draw one that is similar. You will need to decide which tools to use.
• Draw a new and different door design of your own.
• Make a collage of black and white cut out shapes to design a door on a grey piece of paper.
• Use paint, glue, card, corrugated paper, art straws and other reclaimed materials to create a door on a cereal box that has been covered with white paper.

Extending the Ideas 9
The Rainbow Tool

Tools to Use:

Pencil	Square Brush	Round Brush
Spray	Star	Rainbow	Tint Brush

216 Colour Palette

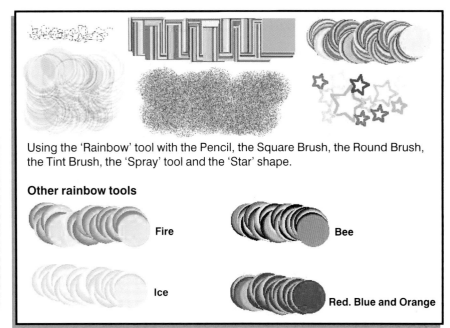

Using the 'Rainbow' tool with the Pencil, the Square Brush, the Round Brush, the Tint Brush, the 'Spray' tool and the 'Star' shape.

Other rainbow tools

Fire

Bee

Ice

Red. Blue and Orange

Talk About

• What the rainbow tool looks like and where it is on the toolbar.
• How to use the rainbow tool (see below).
• Obtaining the other rainbow tools and discovering what they are called - Bee, Ice, Fire, Red Blue and Orange.
• Making and naming a new rainbow tool.
• How to cancel the rainbow tool - by clicking on it with the left mouse button when a drawing has been completed.

Doing

• Left click on the pencil on the toolbar, then left click on the rainbow tool, return to the screen and draw several lines - they should be multi-coloured.
• Left click on the square brush, return to the screen and draw a line - this too should be multicoloured.
• Click on the round brush, the tint brush and the spray gun in turn and draw lines with them - all the lines drawn should be multicoloured.
• Left click on the star tool (see page 44) and drag out a star shape on the screen. Move to another part of the screen, click and drag out another star shape, this one should be a different colour from the first. Continue drawing further stars in the same way - each one should be a different colour from the one before. The box at the end of the colour palette will change colour automatically after each star has been drawn to indicate the colour that the next star will be.
• Left click the rainbow tool to cancel its operation.
• Right click the rainbow tool to explore the other types available. Use the down arrow to select from Rainbow, Fire, Ice, Bee, Red/Blue/Orange. Experiment with each of these on your screen.

• New and individual rainbow tools can also be made. Click on the rainbow tool on the tool bar with the right mouse button, then click on the down arrow until the word 'Blank' appears in the box with a row of grey and white boxes underneath. Go to the 216 colour palette, which should be on the screen, choose and click on a colour with the left mouse button, move to the first grey box, position the arrow that appears inside it, click the left mouse button and the colour you have chosen will replace the grey in the box.
• Click on further colours in turn and fill the other grey boxes in the same way. When all the boxes are full this new rainbow tool needs a name. Highlight and delete the word 'Blank' and type in the name of the new rainbow tool.
• Test your new rainbow tool with the round brush. This new rainbow tool will remain with the others whilst you are using the programme. It will disappear once Dazzle has been shut down.

Extending the Activity

• Explore drawing a repeating pattern of lines and shapes using the rainbow tool.
• Draw a small pattern; use the select area tool and 'Tile' in the 'Area' menu to tile your rainbow design.
• Use thick layers of wax crayon to randomly cover a piece of card. Cover this multicoloured layer with a layer of black. Use the edge of a pair of scissors to draw and scratch through the black to reveal the coloured layer and make a multicoloured drawing.
• Draw randomly in felt tip pen to cover a piece of card. Make a drawing of e.g. a house on a piece of press print. Ink up the press print in black and press it on to the piece of card to make a multicoloured print.

Extending the Ideas 10

Bees and Flowers

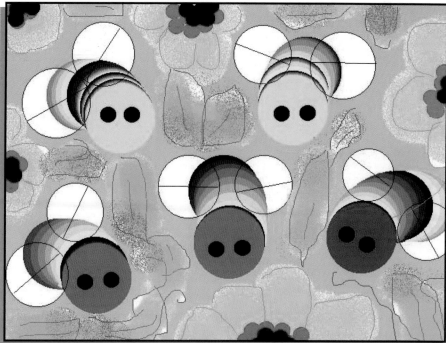

Tools to Use:

Circle	Round Brush	Rainbow
Pencil	Line	Undo	Fill

216 Colour Palette

Talk About

- How to get the 'Bee' rainbow tool.
- How to rectify a mistake using the undo tool.
- How to make the round brush bigger and smaller using the left and right mouse buttons.
- How to make the line tool thinner using the left and right mouse buttons.

Doing

- Left click the fill tool. Left click on a pale shade of green from the colour palette. Left click on the screen to fill it with colour.
- Right click the round brush tool. Increase the size to 100 pt. Left click white on the colour palette. Return to the screen to draw pairs of large white dots about (5 pairs in total) with a gap in between them as wings for the bees.
- Right click the rainbow tool and scroll down beside the word 'Name' until the word 'Bee' appears in the box, click on O.K. and return to the screen.
- Click the left mouse button and drag a bee coloured line/shape between each pair of wings as a body for each bee. As the round brush is still on 100 pt these will be quite thick. Click on the rainbow tool on the tool bar with the left mouse button to stop using it.
- Right click the round brush tool. Decrease the size to 20 pt. Click on close, return to the screen, click on the colour black, then move on to the head of each bee in turn and click and let go the left mouse button to add a pair of eyes to each one.
- Right click the circle tool and use the arrows to create a fine line. Click close and then draw fine circle outlines around each of the white wings.

- Select the line tool and draw a fine line across each wing.
- Select the spray tool and move to the colour palette. Click on a different shade of green and use it to spray some leaf shapes between the bees. Add a third shade of green as well and some yellow shapes as flower petals.
- Click on the round brush on the tool bar with the right mouse button to check that it is still on 20 pt. Return to the screen and click on a shade of red and then black to add dots as the centres of the flowers.
- Left click the pencil tool, click on red, return to the screen and draw lines to outline the petal shapes. Then click on a dark green and draw lines to outline the leaves.
- Save the work on a disc before printing it out. (see pages 5 and 6).

Extending the Activity

- Draw a similar group of bees in a garden full of multicoloured flowers.
- Draw several bees sitting on one large flower head.
- Make a new rainbow tool using different shades of yellow and brown, give it a new name and use it to draw a bee picture of your own.
- Make observational drawings of minibeasts.
- Use a view-finder to zoom in on a picture of a butterfly's wing. Copy the shapes and colours you see in wax crayon on a large (A4 size) piece of paper.

Exploring Radial Lines

Tools to Use:

Line

Radial Lines

Rainbow

Undo

216 Colour Palette

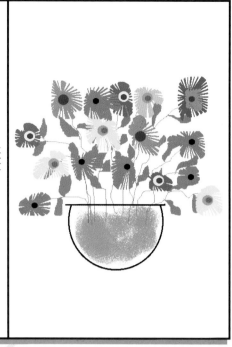

Talk About

- What the radial line tool looks like, where to find it on the toolbar and how to select it.
- How to use the undo tool to rectify a mistake.
- How to make the line tool thicker (which will also alter the thickness of the radial lines) using the left and right mouse buttons.
- Drawing radial lines of one colour on top of radial lines of another colour.

Doing

- Click on the radial line tool on the tool bar with the left mouse button. Return to the screen and click on a red in the colour palette.
- Go back to the screen, position the cross that appears where you want to start drawing, click the left mouse button and drag out a line to the length required then click and hold down the left mouse button whilst dragging the mouse in a circle to create a swirl of radial lines. If you decrease the length of the line whilst you are drawing the radial lines will become shorter.
- Click the right mouse button to finish.
- Experiment further with this tool in the following ways:
- Draw a swirl of radial lines in one colour, then click on a second colour and use this to draw a new swirl on top of the first one. Add a third swirl in another colour on top of both of the other swirls. Draw several small swirls using a different shade of the same colour family e.g. blue for each swirl.
- Click on the rainbow line tool after clicking on the radial line tool and draw a swirl of rainbow radial lines. Draw several swirls of different colours on top of a swirl of rainbow lines.

- Increase the thickness of the radial lines by clicking on the radial line tool with the right mouse button and then clicking the left mouse button on the up arrow to increase the thickness of the line. Click on close when the line is the required thickness. Go back to the screen to draw radial lines as before. This time the lines will be much thicker. Draw a group of these thicker radial lines in different shades of green.

Extending the Activity

- Draw a design of overlapping groups of radial lines of different lengths using three colours only e.g. orange, yellow and black. Use these colours on top of each other in different combinations.
- Use radial lines to create swirls as flower heads. Use the round brush reduced in size to add a dot to the centre of each one. Use the pencil to draw stems and leaves. Use the fill tool to add green to the inside of each leaf. Draw a vase by using the circle shape, rubbing out the top of the circle using the square brush as a rubber after clicking on white and then using the line tool to draw a straight line to join both sides of the circle as the top of the vase. Use a shade of blue and the spray gun to add water inside the vase.
- Press the edge of a thin strip of card dipped in paint on to paper and swirl it round to create in a series of circles of different colours.
- Print straight lines in groups similar to radial lines using the edge of a thin strip of card. Print a centre in each group using a finger dipped in paint and turn the groups of lines into flower heads.

Just a Jungle

Tools to Use:

Spray   Radial Lines   Line

Undo   Pencil   Round Brush

Colours

216 Colour Palette

Talk About
- How to make radial lines thicker (see page 63).
- How to make the round brush thinner (see page 8).
- How to use the undo tool to rectify a mistake (see page 5).
- The range of colours and shapes to use for a jungle picture - look at photographs of jungles and jungle pictures by the artist Henri Rousseau.

Doing
- Click on the spray gun on the toolbar with the left mouse button and return to the screen. Click on a light shade of green on the colour palette with the left mouse button, go back to the screen and add a spray of green all over.
- Click on several other shades of green in turn in the same way and spray them over the screen as well.
- Click on the line tool on the toolbar with the right mouse button, use the left mouse button to click on the up arrow to make the line in the box thicker. Click on Close when the line is the required thickness.
- Click on radial lines with the left mouse button, return to the screen and click on a dark green on the colour palette with the left mouse button. Move to each corner of the screen in turn, click the left mouse button, drag out a line, click and hold down the left mouse button and move the mouse in a circle to create a swirl of thick radial lines. Click right to finish drawing.
- Now reduce the line thickness and pick another shade of green from the colour palette. Move to each corner of the screen in turn and add a swirl of radial lines on top of the previous ones.
- Add further swirls of radial lines on top of the others

using brown, orange and yellow. Make the lines in some of the swirls longer than those in others.
- Click on the round brush on the toolbar with the right mouse button and reduce the size of the brush to 10 pt. Click on close, return to the screen and click on a shade of pale green on the colour palette with the left mouse button.
- Return to the space in the middle of the screen between the groups of radial lines, click the left mouse button and draw lines that twist and curl across the screen.
- Click on other shades of green and add further lines that twist and curl across and next to the first group.
- Finally click on the pencil on the toolbar with the left mouse button, return to the screen, click on a dark green on the colour palette and add some thin twisting and curling lines to the group in the middle of the screen.
- Save the work on a disk before printing it out (see page 6).

Extending the Activity
- Draw a different jungle picture using the same group of tools.
- Draw a jungle picture using a different range of tools.
- Make observational paintings of a group of house plants copying the shapes and mixing the colours as accurately as possible.
- Paint thin strips of paper in different shades of green (about 4 in each shade) and once the strips are dry, use them to make a weaving of a colour family of greens. Mix the different shades together as you weave for added interest.

Extending the Ideas 13

Draw a Garden

Tools to Use:

Spray · Radial Lines · Fill · Star · Undo · Pencil · Round Brush · Wash Brush

216 Colour Palette

Talk About

- The new tool to use - the wash brush - what it looks like and where it is found on the toolbar.
- What the wash brush will do - merge and blur colours together.
- The different shapes and colours of groups of flowers in a garden - pictures and photographs will be needed as a stimulus for this.

Doing

- Click on the fill tool with the left mouse button, move to the screen and click on a pale shade of green on the colour palette with the left mouse button. Return to the screen, click the left mouse button and the screen will fill with green.
- Click on the spray gun with the left mouse button, move to the colour palette, click on another shade of green then click the left mouse button, spray and add patches of this green to different parts of the screen. Use another shade of green as well if you want.
- The flowers in this picture were drawn using a range of colours and tools. The blue and white flowers and the small pink flowers were drawn using the spray gun. The pink and orange flowers next to them were drawn using the round brush reduced to 25 pt using the left and right mouse buttons. The wash brush on the toolbar was then clicked on with the left mouse button. On returning to the screen the brush and circle that appeared were positioned on the pink and orange flowers. The left mouse button was then clicked on different parts of the flowers. This made the colours mix and blur together.
- Radial lines were used to draw other groups of flowers. The yellow and green flowers at the top

left-hand side were drawn using the round brush that had been reduced to 10 pt using the left and right mouse buttons. The small orange flowers next to them were drawn using the star shape.
- The flowers at the top on the left hand side were drawn using the wash brush, first to blur and blend some of the greens in the background together, then yellow and white dots were added on top using the round brush reduced to size 10 pt. White petals were drawn and added using the pencil.
- Dots were added to the centre of the flowers using the round brush reduced to 15 pt for the larger flowers and then to 6 pt for the smaller ones.
- The leaves and stems were drawn using a dark green from the colour palette and the pencil.
- The fill tool and another shade of green were used to add colour inside each of the leaf shapes. When doing this if the green fill spreads outside any of the leaves it means that the outline of the leaf is incomplete. Click on the undo tool to rectify the mistake, redraw and extend the outline of the leaf using the pencil before using the fill tool again.
- Save the work on disk before printing it out.

Extending the Activity

- Draw another garden using different tools and different colours.
- Create a torn strip tissue paper collage garden on a rectangle of white paper- A4 size. Add flower heads to the collage in cut and torn paper shapes and printing with strips of card, finger prints and cotton wool buds.
- Look at paintings of gardens by Gustav Klimt, Vincent Van Gogh or Claude Monet. Paint a picture of a garden featured in a photograph in the style of one of these artists.

Egyptian Collars

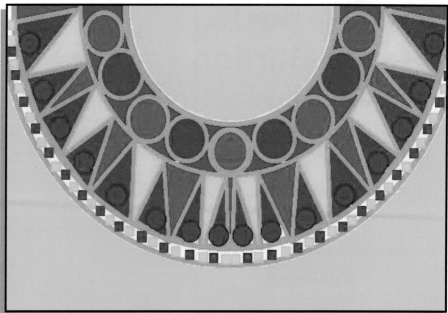

Tools to Use:

Circle   Square Brush   Fill

Undo   Line   Zoom

216 Colour Palette

Talk About

• The new tool to use - the zoom tool - and what it will do (go in closely to part of the screen to allow small spaces to be filled or added to accurately).
• How to use the zoom tool (see below).
• How to use the undo tool to rectify a mistake.
• How to reduce the size of the round brush and the square brush using the left and right mouse buttons, (see page 8).
• Pictures of Egyptian collars- the shapes and colours used in their design.

Doing

• Click on the circle tool with the left mouse button. Return to the screen and position the cross that appears at the top of the screen in the middle. Click the left mouse button, let go and drag out a circle shape downwards from the top of the screen. Make the circle quite large so that it becomes a semi-circle across the top of the screen. Left click to finish drawing.
• Continue using the circle tool in the same way to drag out further semi-circles underneath the first one creating the shape of a collar.
• To fill and decorate the collar use the circle tool, the round brush reduced in size, the square brush reduced in size and the line tool to add shapes between the semi-circle shapes.
• Choose and click on colours from the colour palette that match those found on the Egyptian collars in pictures when drawing with the tools and also when filling in any gaps.
• If some small gaps in between the shapes on the collar fail to fill when the fill tool is used, click on the zoom tool on the toolbar with the left mouse button, move back to the screen and position the magnifying glass on the part to be filled. Click the left mouse button and the part to be filled will be enlarged. Click on the fill tool, then click on the colour to be used, move back to the collar. Position the arrow that appears on the part to be filled and keep clicking the left mouse button on the gaps to fill them.
• When the gap in the collar is filled, click on the screen with the right mouse button and the whole collar will reduce in size.
• Zoom in on any other gaps that need filling in the same way.
• Finally use the fill tool, and a pale shade of green from the colour palette to fill the screen area above and below the completed collar.

Extending the Activity

• Draw a further collar using the same shapes arranged in a different way.
• Draw another collar using different shapes to fill the spaces in the collar.
• Make a collage of an Egyptian collar using different papers and foils - in Egyptian colours. Draw the semi-circle shapes first with a felt tip pen.
• Make an Egyptian collar using wooden clothes pegs and a broad semi-circle of card. Clip the pegs around and protruding from the outer edge of the semi-circle card collar. Decorate the pegs with cut paper and foil shapes and patterns using felt tip pens - all in Egyptian colours.

Extending the Ideas 15
Moving Figures

Tools to Use:

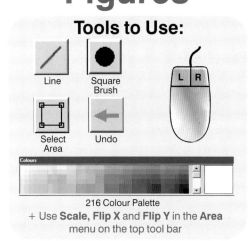

Line   Square Brush

Select Area   Undo

L   R

Colours

216 Colour Palette
+ Use **Scale, Flip X** and **Flip Y** in the **Area** menu on the top tool bar

Moving figures scaled

Figures flipped X

Figures flipped Y

Talk About
- Different ways of moving about and the positions that arms, legs and bodies get into during these different movements.
- Simple figures in pictures by L.S. Lowry and the different movements they show.
- How to reduce the size of the figures (see below).
- How Flip X will reverse the figures from left to right and Flip Y will turn the figures upside down.

Doing
- Make some quick sketches of simple linear moving figures in a sketchbook similar to the examples above.
- Left click the round brush tool, select black from the colour palette and left click on the page four times to make four black filled circles for heads.
- Right click on the line tool and use the up arrow to increase the thickness of the line. Left click to close the box. Now left click at the base of the first head and drag a line down to create a body. Remember, left click allows you to change direction, right click cuts off your line at the point you have reached. In this way, draw line bodies for the four heads.
- Click on the select area tool with the left mouse button, return to the screen and position the cross that appears close to the first figure at the top on the left-hand side. Click the left mouse button, hold it down and drag out a box around the figure, don't click or you will lose the box but left click 'Area' on the top toolbar. Left click 'Scale'.
- Return to the screen, the box around the figure will now have disappeared. Position the cross that appears in a space on the screen, click and hold down the left mouse button and drag out a small red box, click the left mouse button to finish and

the figure that was in the first box will now appear reduced to the size of the small box you drew. The large version of the same figure will still be on the screen.
- Reduce the size of the other figures in the same way until you have a large and small version of each on the screen.
- Save the work on a disk before printing it out. (see page 6).
- Reload the work, use the select area tool as before to draw a box around a figure - either a large or a small one - (don't click or you will lose the box), but move to 'Area' on the top tool bar, scroll down to 'Flip X' and click the left mouse button. The figure you put the box round will now be facing the opposite way. Change the directions so that some of the other figures face in the same way.
- Use the above process again, this time selecting Flip Y.
- The screen should eventually be full of large and small figures facing different directions.
- Print the work and save it on disk under a new name.

Extending the Activity
- Arrange some of the figures in groups using the select area tool and 'Move' in the 'Area' menu on the top tool bar.
- Duplicate some of the figures in groups using the area tool and 'Copy' in the 'Area' menu on the top tool bar.
- Make drawings of moving figures in the playground 'Lowry Style'.
- Copy the figures in a newspaper picture of a sports activity 'Lowry Style' but in modern clothes.

Camouflage Patterns

Tools to Use:

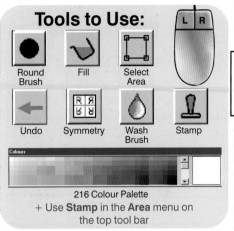

Round Brush	Fill	Select Area
Undo	Symmetry	Wash Brush	Stamp

216 Colour Palette

+ Use **Stamp** in the **Area** menu on the top tool bar

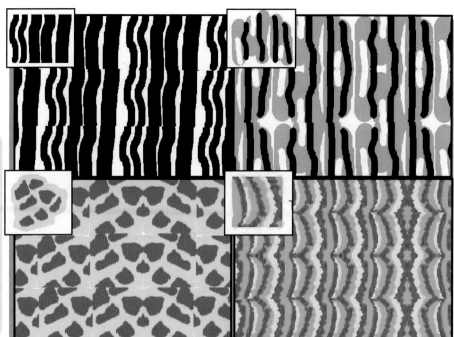

Talk About

- How to get the different types of symmetry (see below).
- How to find 'Stamp' in the 'Area' menu on the top tool bar.
- How to stop using 'Stamp' by clicking on select area tool.

Doing

The Zebra Pattern

- Click on the round brush and use black to draw a small group of thick and thin parallel lines.
- Left click the select area tool and drag a tight box around your pattern.
- Left click 'Area' on the top tool bar and select 'Stamp' from the drop down menu.
- Return to the screen and stamp the pattern by left clicking. To stop stamping, left click on the select area tool.

The Tiger Pattern

- Click on the round brush and use orange, black and white in turn to draw a small group of thick and thin overlapping lines.
- Right click the symmetry tool. Left click on the tick next to up/down symmetry followed by O.K.
- Left click the select area tool and drag a tight box around your pattern.
- Left click 'Area' on the top tool bar and select 'Stamp' from the drop down menu.
- Return to the screen and stamp the pattern by left clicking. Because 'up/down' symmetry is on the screen the pattern will appear in two places each time it is stamped. To stop stamping, left click on the select area tool.

The Giraffe Pattern

- Draw small outline shapes in yellow using a reduced round brush, then fill the shapes using brown and the fill tool.
- Right click the symmetry tool. Left click to place a tick next to up/down symmetry plus an empty box next to left/right followed by O.K.
- Left click the select area tool and drag a tight box around your pattern.
- Left click 'Area' on the top tool bar and select 'Stamp' from the drop down menu.
- Return to the screen and stamp the pattern by left clicking. Because 'left/right' symmetry is on the screen the pattern will appear in two places each time it is stamped. To stop stamping, left click on the select area tool.

The Snake Pattern

- Draw this using yellow, two shades of green and a thin round brush.
- Right click the symmetry tool. Left click to place a tick next to up/down symmetry plus a tick next to left/right followed by O.K.
- Left click the select area tool and drag a tight box around your pattern.
- Left click 'Area' on the top tool bar and select 'Stamp' from the drop down menu.
- Return to the screen and stamp the pattern by left clicking. Because four-way symmetry is on the screen the pattern will appear in four places each time it is stamped. To stop stamping, left click on the select area tool.

Extending the Activity

- Explore drawing small patterns of your own design to stamp and use a different type of symmetry with each one.
- Try drawing a flower using the round brush and the colours black, yellow, blue and purple. Click on the wash brush tool with the left mouse button and use it to blur some of the colours together. Use this to stamp a pattern. Try varying the size of flowers using the scale tool in the 'Area' drop down menu.
- Cut a piece of coloured magazine in the middle of a piece of paper and use wax crayon to match the colours and extend the shapes to camouflage the original piece of magazine.

Extending the Ideas 17
Illuminated Letters

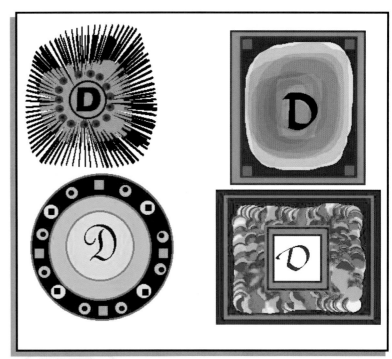

Tools to Use:

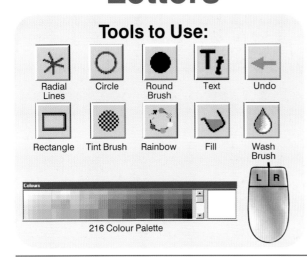

Radial Lines	Circle	Round Brush	Text	Undo
Rectangle	Tint Brush	Rainbow	Fill	Wash Brush

Colours

216 Colour Palette

L R

Talk About
- What illuminated letters look like, the shapes used to decorate them and how these shapes are arranged - examples of illuminated letters will be needed for this.
- How to make the round brush and the square brush thicker and thinner.
- How to change the font and the letter size.
- How to rectify a mistake using the undo tool.

Doing
Design 1 (top left)
- Left click the radial lines tool and select the colour black to create a swirl of black lines. Repeat making shorter lines with the colour orange.
- Left click the circle tool and select the colour black to draw a circle in the centre. Surround this with brown dots using the round brush at 20 pt. Add black dots to the centre of these at 5 pt.
- Right click the text tool and use the arrows to select a font you like and size 48 or 72 pt. Left click O.K. and move the cursor to the centre of your design before typing in a letter of your choice.

Design 2 (top right)
- The centre was created using the tint brush and different shades of pink and purple. This shape was then surrounded by two rectangles of different sizes using the rectangle shape. The fill tool plus pink and purple were used to add colour around the tinted shape and between the rectangles. The square brush was reduced in size to about 10 pt and used to add squares to each corner of the inner rectangle. The font for the letter and its size were chosen in the same way as before.

Design 3 (bottom left)
- The third design was created using the circle tool to draw several circles of different sizes inside one another and filling them with different colours - yellow, orange and black. The round brush was reduced in size to 25 pt and used to add circles around the inside edge of the outer circle. The square brush was reduced to 10 pt and clicked and used to add small squares to the top, bottom, left and right of the outer circle. The font for the letter and its size were chosen in the same way as before.

Design 4 (bottom right)
- The final design was created using the rainbow tool and the round brush, size 20 pt, to create a shape. The colours were then blurred slightly using the wash brush. The rectangle tool was then used to surround the shape with several rectangles of different sizes and to add further small rectangles to the centre of the design. The fill tool plus dark blue, red and white were used to fill these rectangles. The font for the letter and its size were chosen in the same way using the text tool.

Extending the Activity
- Use different tools and colours to design new illuminated letters.
- Produce a design for both your own initials.
- Use a letter template to draw round, or a large letter cut from a newspaper or magazine. Cut out paper shapes and draw with felt tip pen to decorate them.

Extending the Ideas 18
Drawing Ruins

Tools to Use:

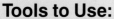

Spray

Square Brush

Pencil

Undo

L R

Colours

216 Colour Palette

Stage 1

Stage 2

Stage 3

Talk About
- What the words mood and atmosphere mean in the context of a picture.
- Pictures of ruins and work by the artist John Piper would be useful stimulus material for this activity. Talk about the mood and atmosphere such pictures evoke - and why.
- How to use the undo tool to rectify a mistake. There are three illustrations for this work that show the different stages from start to finish in the making of this drawing.

Doing
- In a sketch book, using crayon or coloured pencil, collect the colours used in the stimulus pictures of ruins to create mood and atmosphere - they will probably be quite dark e.g. grey, black, dark blue and dark green etc.

Stage 1
- Click on the spray gun tool with the left mouse button then click on each of the colours you found in turn and use them to spray across and cover the screen. Spray paler and less colour at the top of the screen, and darker colours at the bottom - remember you can always add more colour later.

Stage 2
- Click on the square brush tool with the left mouse button and choose one of the colours from the palette (black has been used in the example) return to the screen. Click and move the mouse to make filled squares and use these squares to build the shape of part of a ruin. The outline should be irregular and have pieces missing. Leave gaps where there could be doors. Click on a second colour (cream has been used in the example) and add a further unfinished shape in the same way to the ruins. Continue adding further shapes using other colours e.g. grey and brown. Add smaller shapes, as crumbling walls at the bottom part of the drawing.

Stage 3
- Click on the pencil tool with the left mouse button and use this to add linear drawing to each of the ruins in turn. This drawing should add details such as brick shapes and windows. Outline some of the ruins and add more drawing to turn the doorways into arches. Try drawing lines close together and on top of each other in some places for added interest. Use different colours for this linear drawing from your original collection e.g. black, white and brown on top the various colours used for the ruins; brown on top of black etc.
- Return to use the spray gun and gently add bursts of darker colour to the sky above the ruins. Rectify any mistakes e.g. if you accidentally spray on top of the ruins rather than around and above them, by using the undo tool immediately - remember it will only undo your last move.
- Save the work on disk and print it out.

Extending the Activity
- Draw a similar group of ruins but colour the sky as if it is a sunset - look at pictures of sunsets and collect the colours you need in your sketchbook first.
- Draw a similar group of ruins but turn it into a snow scene - look at pictures of snow scenes and collect the colours you need in your sketchbook first.
- Explore mixing in paint the colours you used for your drawing of ruins and use them to make a painting of the school or the local environment.
- Make a torn paper collage of ruins using the same colours as in your drawing. Use a sponge dipped in paint to add the background.

Drawing a Landscape

Tools to Use:

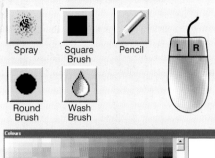

Spray
Square Brush
Pencil

Round Brush
Wash Brush

L R

216 Colour Palette

Stage 1

Stage 2

Stage 3

Talk About

- What foreground, middle-ground and distance mean and differentiating these in pictures of landscapes in colour magazines.
- That detail can be seen clearly in the foreground, less so in the middle-ground and not at all in the distance.
- That colour is stronger in the foreground and paler in the distance.
- Which tools to use, where they are found and how to get them from the tool bar.
- How to make the round and square brush thicker and thinner using the left and right mouse buttons (see page 8).
- How to use the undo tool to rectify a mistake.
  There are three illustrations for this work that show different stages from start to finish in the making of this drawing.

Doing

- In a sketchbook, using crayon or coloured pencils, collect the colours needed for a landscape drawing.

Stage 1

- Click on the spray gun with the left mouse button and use different shades of green to draw the outline shape of the hills and to spray across and cover the working area. Spray a darker band of green across the middle of the scene as trees, and spray shades of grey as the sky between the shapes of the hills. If the sky becomes too dark spray some white to lighten it.

Stage 2

- Click on the square brush with the right mouse button and reduce its size to 25 pt. Return to the screen and click squares in grey, black and orange in turn to draw a low wall across the screen below the row of trees.
- Click on the wash brush with the left mouse button and use it to blur and blend some of the colours on the wall together.

Stage 3

- Click on the pencil tool with the left mouse button and use it to add linear drawing and detail to the landscape e.g. outline and add further sloping lines to the hills. Add an outline and branches to the row of trees and draw the outline of stones of different sizes on the wall. Use black, white and grey.
- Click on the round brush with the right mouse button and use the left mouse button to reduce its size to 10 pt. Click on different greens and draw lots of vertical overlapping lines as grass across the screen under the wall. Use the pencil tool and black and white to add further vertical lines.
- Use the round brush (size 10 pt) plus the colour white to click and add dots as flowers, in groups, across the screen underneath the long grass. Increase the size of the round brush to 16 pt, click on yellow then click and add more dots as flowers, in groups, across the scene between the groups of white dots.
- Save the work on disk and print it out.

Extending the Activity

- Use the same tools to draw a picture of a seascape (look at magazine pictures first) and remember to consider what is needed for the foreground, middle-ground and distance.
- Use the same tools to draw a picture of the view from a window at school. Make a rough drawing in a sketchbook first - look carefully at the foreground, middle-ground and distance as you draw.
- Develop the sketch of the view from the window at school into a large - scale painting. Overdraw with oil pastel to add details to the painting.

Extending the Ideas 20
The Grey Scale Palette

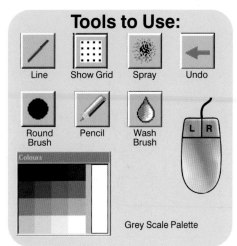

Tools to Use:

Line Show Grid Spray Undo

Round Brush Pencil Wash Brush

L R

Colours

Grey Scale Palette

Talk About

- How to get the 16 Grey Scale Palette (see page 51).
- How to use the grey scale palette to create depth and distance i.e. use the darker shades in the foreground, gradually introducing some paler shades. Keep the palest shades for the distance.
- Remember objects in the foreground will be larger and more detailed than objects in the distance.

Doing

To draw a picture of a Wood (see above).

- Click on the spray gun with the left mouse button. Click on a dark shade on the grey scale palette and click and spray across the bottom of the screen. Click on a paler shade and click and spray that further up the screen. Complete the spraying with a very pale shade. Click on the round brush with the left mouse button, click on a dark shade on the grey scale palette and draw three trees in the foreground. Right click the round brush and reduce its size. Click on a paler shade and draw a couple of trees in the middle ground. Reduce the size of the round brush tool again, select an even paler shade and draw three trees in the distance. Click on the pencil tool and use black to draw some fine lines as the horizon and then white to add details to the trees in the foreground. Spray some darker shades around the branches and across the tops of the trees. Save the work on disk and print it out.

To draw a picture of a view through a window (see front cover).

- Click on the spray gun with the left mouse button and spray several shades of pale grey across the top of the screen. Click on the wash brush tool and use it to blur the shades together to create clouds. Spray pale grey under the clouds down to the bottom of the screen and spray dark grey on either side of the screen as trees. Click on the pencil tool and use it with black to draw a fence in the distance and to add texture to each of the trees. Click on the round brush tool with the right mouse button and use the left mouse button to reduce it to 20 pt. Draw a fence across the screen between the trees. Left click on the pencil tool then click on the colour white to add lines and highlight the fence posts. Click on the line tool with right mouse button, make the line thicker, return to the screen and still using black, draw vertical and horizontal lines across the screen to create a window frame. Click on the pencil tool with the left mouse button and use it with black to draw tiles as the widow sill. Save the work on disk and print it out.

Extending the Activity

- Look at landscape pictures in magazines, make a rough drawing of the main shapes in one of them in a sketchbook before turning it into a tonal drawing on the computer.
- Make a drawing of an imaginary landscape using different tones.
- Make an observational pencil drawing of a view around the school - use different tones to create depth, detail and interest.